Self-Editing for Self-Publishers

by

Derrick & Sarah Grant

KENNEBEC
PUBLISHING

Self-Editing for Self-Publishers
Copyright 2017
Kennebec Publishing, LLC
ISBN: 978-1-939473-59-2
Printed in the United States of America.

Contents

Introduction 1
   The choice to go it alone 3
PART I: EDITING 101 7
   Types of editing 7
   Resources 9
   Books 9
   Elements of style 10
   On writing 10
   Grammar girl's quick and dirty tips 10
   for better writing 10
   The Chicago Manual of Style 11
   The Associated Press Stylebook 11
   Electronic resources 12
   Spell check 12
   Grammar check 12
   Find and replace 13
   Grammarly 13
   Purdue OWL 14
   Scrivener 14
   Hemingway App 15
   Consistency checker 15
   Common errors to look for 16

PART TWO:
THE EDITING PROCESS 29
   Step one: Take a break 29
   Step two: Listen to your book 30
   Step three: Check for narrative and character arc 34

   Step four: Check consistency 41

   Step five: Fact-check 50

   Step six: Improve your writing 54

   Step seven: Check your chapters 66
   Step eight: Proofread 70

Step nine: Print it 78
Step ten (optional): Read it backward 81
PART III:
THE FINISHED PRODUCT 84
Conclusion 89

Introduction

So you've done it. You've written a masterpiece, a work of your own, and now you're considering self-publishing. First, congratulations! It takes creativity, effort, motivation, and diligence to write a book. Heck, it takes a lot of effort and motivation to write anything, let alone a book. Sometimes it can feel like the words just won't come, but when you push through, keep writing, and are able to finish what you started, it truly is an accomplishment to be proud of.

However, your work isn't over once you've finished writing. Sorry to burst your bubble, but if you want to publish a quality work, there is more to do. Editing and proofreading may not be as fun as putting a story on paper, but these steps are crucial to the writing and publishing process. Cleaning up your writing with a bright red pen is especially important if you are self-publishing, as you won't have a publishing house to provide you with critical feedback or a keen eye to catch missing punctuation or the *your* where *you're* should be.

Don't despair! With the right tools and guidance, you can proofread and edit your book yourself, utilize the help of family and friends, or even find a relatively affordable editor to do a final spot-check after you've done a round of editing. Try to look at editing your book as putting the wax on your car. You want it to look the best it can be, right? You want it polished. With this "fine touch" attitude, editing won't seem like as much of a chore, and you may even come to enjoy it!

Sure, aspects of editing are always going to be tedious. Rough writing is freeform. Editing is formal. It means thinking critically, and improving your own work. Often, it can mean deleting or completely rewriting entire sections of a manuscript that you have sweated over. Ouch. There's a reason Ernest Hemingway said editing should be done sober. Editing means paying attention to details.

Self-editing is even more painful than editing someone else's work because you are tearing up your own words. It's one instance, though, in which the natural human tendency to be our own worst critic can actually be of great use. Just don't overdo it, or, as you'll read about toward the end of this book, you'll edits your edits and never stop.

Of course, there's an easy way out of the time-consuming and sometimes downright painful act of self-editing, but like most easy ways out, it costs money. Professional editing services exist, but they can be expensive. Before you take that route, give yourself a chance. If you've taken the time and made the effort to write a book, you likely have the discipline to self-edit. Creative minds might need a little more of a push and a lot more guidance to undertake an effective, focused editing process. However, if you can write, you can edit, and it just might improve your writing on the whole.

We know that self-editing can seem overwhelming. That's why we're writing this book (a book we have self-edited), so you can gain the tools to self-edit your writing. We've provided a list of resources for you to take a look at before you start, and those will serve as your Bibles as you edit. We've also broken down the editing process into steps that you can follow in sequential order or pick and choose in a way that works for you. We've even included what we hope are some simple explanations of common errors and how to fix them. You still have to do the hard work, but knowing where to start, what to do, and where to find useful tools and resources will put you way ahead of the game. We've also included helpful grammar tips throughout this book, focused on some of the most common issues writers encounter.

Think you don't have the time to self-edit? You had the time to write the book. Think you just can't do it? You can. Take it one step at a time. Like anything in life that seems just too big to tackle, when you break up the task of self-editing into smaller tasks and more manageable chunks, it becomes less of a beast to tackle and more of housecat to tame.

Self-editing is not easy, and it's not quick. But self-editing is possible, and it can be of great benefit for you and your writing skills.

THE CHOICE TO GO IT ALONE

Let's get the negative stuff out of the way at the beginning—the risks of self-editing. Yes, there are risks to consider when you decide to self-edit your work. First and foremost, you know your work too well. You know exactly what you intend to say, and where the story is going. You know what your characters are like (or are supposed to be like) and what their backstories are. You know everything about the town or planet where your story is set, and you know how it got that way. So why is this intimate familiarity a problem?

It's a problem because you won't spot what might confuse the reader. You will be able to understand even the most awkward of sentences because you wrote them, and you know their underlying meaning. As a result, when you're editing your own work you are likely to miss grammatical errors, plot holes, chronology or time errors, as well as opportunities to improve your writing style. You'll read right over them.

There's a good chance you've been living and breathing this work for months, possibly years. By the time the editing process comes around, you may be very tired of the book. The thought of reading the story and the same words over again after you've "finished" is just daunting. This may cause you to skim over parts and move more quickly than you should.

It is possible to avoid these risks by taking a careful, disciplined approach to the self-editing process. We lay out the tactics for doing so in this book, offering tips, tricks, and strategies for approaching the process and avoiding pitfalls. However, if discipline isn't one of your strengths, you might want to consider if self-editing is right for you. But, even if you decide the entire self-editing process isn't for you, you should at least take a first crack at editing your book before shipping it off to a professional editor or proofreader. Any polishing you can do will cut down on the number of hours they have to spend on it (and that you have to pay for). It will also make you look better if you aren't sending a manuscript full of typos for them to laugh or sigh at.

Alright, enough with the negativity. Let's talk about the rewards of self-editing. Believe it or not, there are plenty of benefits for putting yourself through this rigorous process. Perhaps most important for many people trying to earn a living from their writing, it's far cheaper than hiring a professional editor or proofreader.

The Editorial Freelancers Association's website (the-efa.org) shows that common rates for editing services range anywhere from $30-$60 an hour depending on the type of editing. If an editor completes seven pages an hour, and you have written a 210-page book, then the minimum amount you can expect to pay for a solid editing job is $900!

The Writer's Market reports the average rate for copyediting is $4.10 per page, putting the cost for a 210-page book in the same range as the Editorial Freelancers Association cites.

To put the cost of hiring a professional editor in perspective, $900 is more than the average American's weekly wage. According to the Bureau of Labor Statistics, Americans make $850 per week on average. And many people make much less than that per week. If you live in a big city, $850 is very easily your rent payment for the month, or even just a portion of your rent. Do you have a week's wages or a rent payment or more to spend on hiring someone to do what you can do yourself? And even if you do, is it really worth it? Do you pay someone $60 an hour to do other tasks that you can accomplish with a little bit of focus and elbow grease? Probably not. And this is for just one book. Today's fiction writers are often expected to churn out title after title. For a new author still establishing an audience, it's easy to get priced out of writing quite quickly.

Of course, in this age of the internet, there are cheaper options than paying industry rates, but it's very possible (actually, likely) that you'll end up sacrificing quality and doing a final proofreading job yourself, anyway. On Upwork.com, for example, there are people posting that they are willing to pay only $50 for editing of a 150-page book. Paying that rate to a freelancer won't attract a quality editor, and you'll likely just be wasting your time and your money. What's the point of hiring an editor if you just have to edit their work? Never mind the general hassle of sifting through applications and dealing with possibly dozens that are just a complete waste of your time.

Self-editing from the beginning is clearly the wallet-friendly solution, but frugality isn't the only reason to self-edit. Done right, self-editing also has the added benefit of improving your writing skills. Why? Because you'll begin paying more attention to your writing. As you self-edit, you'll start to notice bad habits you need to break. After you've self-edited a couple hundred pages of your work, you'll notice the words you use too often, the words you regularly misspell, and the grammatical rules you tend to break. Do you tend to add *very* where you shouldn't be adding it (hint: you should almost never be adding *very* into your writing)? You'll notice. Do you start too many sentences with *this* or *these*? You'll notice. Do you have a tendency to write descriptive sentences in a manner that's confusing? You'll notice.

Then, when you sit down to work on your next project, you'll be more conscientious about the errors you picked up during your previous self-editing efforts. Your writing tics will be hard to miss because you have seen them over and over again, and they will be beaten into your head much more effectively than if you have just had an editor tell you that it's a tic you need to correct. You'll be so annoyed with your bad writing habits by the time you finish the self-editing process that you'll never forget them. The next time you sit down to write anything, even an email, you'll balk when you start a sentence with *this*, and then reconsider and revise, making your writing stronger from the get-go. Eventually, thinking in this way won't be a conscious effort at all, but simply how you write. Yes, disciplined and careful self-editing might be tedious, but it certainly will pay off in the long run. If this writing project is only the first of many you hope to undertake, then consider self-editing as furthering your education and career goals. You might even discover you enjoy editing, and be able to earn some of those sweet $60 rates for editing other people's work at some point down the line. See? Self-editing can be well worth the time investment.

PART I: EDITING 101

Since you've now considered the risks and rewards of self-editing and you are still reading, you've presumably determined that the rewards of self-editing outweigh the risks. Great! Let's get started with the nitty-gritty.

TYPES OF EDITING

So, what is editing? "Finding mistakes" is the easy answer, but it's not the full answer. There are different types of editing, all of which you need to understand before you begin going through your manuscript. Let's go over them:

Proofreading is the process of correcting simple errors such as typos or misused punctuation marks. Simple grammar, spelling, and word usage errors (think affect/effect) are also corrected during proofreading. Proofreading also means finding errors in spacing, like when you forget to hit the spacebar hard after a period, so no space appears. Proofreading is very detail-oriented, and can be a slow process. However, it prevents distracting errors from getting into your published work that jump out at readers even if they don't jump out at you on your fourth or fifth reading. Proofreading is absolutely essential to making sure your work looks professional and that you are taken seriously as a writer.

Copyediting goes deeper than proofreading, as it includes not only correcting spelling, grammatical, and punctuation errors, but paying attention to the style and consistency of your writing. Do you underline a book title on one page, but put it in quotes on the next? Do you unnecessarily use the same word repeatedly in the span of one paragraph? Do you refer to one character as Samantha throughout half of a book but all of a sudden change to calling her Sam just for chapter ten? These are the kinds of errors and inconsistencies that copyediting seeks to find. Like proofreading, copyediting requires strict attention to detail and can be a tedious process. However, it pays off when your work is polished and error-free, allowing readers to focus on the strength of your writing and not redundancies and errors that made it into print.

Line editing focuses on your language usage. During a line edit you are looking for ways to improve the manuscript, rather than simply correcting errors. Could you switch out a word for one that is more effective? What about cutting an adverb or revising a sentence's structure to improve clarity? Are your sentences filled with clichés that should be eliminated and replaced with original writing? Line editing may be the most useful form of self-editing if you are hoping to improve your writing through the self-editing process.

Developmental editing addresses the structure of a written work. It might involve moving around entire chapters, revising a character's story arc, or removing entire plot elements. While certain tone and style consistencies can be addressed during line editing and copyediting, ensuring the overall voice and tone of a written work stays consistent falls under developmental editing. Developmental editing can be difficult to undertake when you are editing your own work, as you know the work inside and out, so you have no problem seeing where it's headed or how a certain plot element fits in. However, if you are able to step back and self-edit with a critical, unbiased eye, you will be able to spot plot holes and opportunities for improvement, and you will become a better writer because of it.

When you're self-editing, the different types of editing will overlap during your read-throughs. When you notice a way to improve your writing or see an error, there's no reason to say, "oh, I'll fix that in my proofreading read-through, this is my line editing phase." Fix it when you see it; the different types of editing are a way to focus your work, but they shouldn't remain completely separate. Unlike a large publishing house, you don't have a separate developmental editor and a proofreader; you are reading this book because you are all of the above. So work with the pieces together, the way that works for you.

Okay, now that we've got the different types of editing out of the way, let's delve into what's out there for tools to help you in the self-editing process.

RESOURCES

Even the most seasoned grammar pro will have questions or need a nudge in the right direction when editing. No one truly edits alone; there's an entire history of language usage and tomes on style. A hefty trove of resources, print and electronic, can be both a guiding light and a lifesaver when editing. They can even be inspiring reads in between bouts of editing work (I'm looking at you, Strunk & White). The English language is complicated, and you will undoubtedly run into a situation where you don't know what to do about that comma or semicolon. Thankfully, there are people who have dedicated their lives to putting instructions about grammar and style into manuals and guides. Whether you prefer to look up information online or in a printed book, there is a resource available. Here are some of the most basic and helpful to get you started.

BOOKS

It never hurts to start with the basics—a dictionary and a thesaurus. You can find all of these resources online, but sometimes it is easier to just flip through pages to what you are looking for. Having a hardcopy of a dictionary and a thesaurus is particularly important if you are the type of person who easily falls down internet rabbit holes, and shouldn't open up Google in the middle of an editing project. If you prefer to edit on a hardcopy of your manuscript, having an actual dictionary and an actual thesaurus will also give you the chance to look up definitions and synonyms without having to turn on your computer at all. Plus, having these two volumes sitting on your desk gives your workspace a certain sense of gravitas and professionalism. Just don't use the thesaurus to substitute words with five syllables when a one syllable word will do merely for the sake of sounding intellectual. Brevity, after all, is the soul of wit.

Elements of Style

Strunk & White's *Elements of Style* is practically standard issue for college freshmen studying the liberal arts, and for good reason. The slim volume, originally penned by E.B. White's professor and then expanded upon by the *Charlotte's Web* author, provides "Elementary Rules of Usage," a.k.a. basic grammatical rules, along with style advice and general thoughts on writing that are as insightful as they are entertaining. For example, the book's explanation of the difference between *nauseous* and *nauseated* contains this gem: "Do not, therefore, say 'I feel nauseous,' unless you are sure you have that effect on others." With that zinger, the advice is likely to stick in your head.

On Writing

For general insight into the writing craft, Stephen King's *On Writing* has become a modern favorite among writers. Perhaps the most famous insight he offers in the book is on his least favorite part of speech: "I believe the road to hell is paved with adverbs." Picking up the horror master's memoir is an inspirational and instructive way to take a break between writing and editing. You'll certainly never look at adverbs the same way again.

Grammar Girl's Quick and Dirty Tips for Better Writing

Grammar Girl's Quick and Dirty Tips for Better Writing by Mignon Fogarty is an easy read and a quick reference worth owning. Humorous, peppered with memorable examples, and with detailed explanations of the most common grammar questions, this book is worth picking up even in the midst of your writing process. While it is easy to find the answer to a question that arises while editing, knowing a rule and not having to pause in the middle of writing to consider it will increase the pace at which you work and improve your writing overall.

The Chicago Manual of Style

To counterbalance these modern resources, let's move to an older, stodgier, but highly-revered reference. First published in 1906, *The Chicago Manual of Style* is a comprehensive guide to all things grammatical and stylistic. From when to use a comma, to how to format a book title (italics), this tome is likely to have the answer for whatever obscure question you come up with. And, with a searchable online version now available, you can find an answer more quickly than ever. An annual subscription to www.chicagomanualofstyle.org will run you $35, but the ease of use makes it a worthy investment for an aspiring author. Of course, if you prefer the old-fashioned method of flipping through pages and checking an index, the print book is readily available.

The Associated Press Stylebook

The *Associated Press Stylebook* can be a valuable addition to your reference library. It is easy to use, but as it focuses on usages and styles that journalists use, you might find it most useful if you are working on a nonfiction project.

Here, it's worth noting that when you pick a style guide, you need to stick with it. Don't jump back and forth between the *Chicago Manual of Style* and the *AP Style Guide*. Your work will lack consistency if you do, sometimes causing confusion to the reader, and always making you seem unprofessional.

Electronic Resources

It is the 21st century, so we should consider how technology can assist with the self-editing process. From features integrated with word processing programs, to independent apps, to reference websites, you can find much of what you need online. Let's start with the basics.

Spell Check

We all know how to use Microsoft Word's spell check, and we all know how irritating and distracting the squiggly lines can be when they appear as you're in the middle of typing a key sentence. However, for a first round of self-editing, spell check can be an efficient tool. You just have to use it carefully. Make sure you don't accidentally click to correct a character's name to a common word, or that you get so used to clicking "ignore" that you miss a necessary change. There's also the age-old caution for spell check use that always bears repeating—it doesn't catch homonyms! Your mixed-up *to* and *too* will get by the spell check programs. So will *bare* and *bear*. Bare arms and bear arms are two scarily different concepts. Don't depend on spell check entirely. It would be a breach of the unspoken laws of writing advice for us not to warn you.

Grammar Check

Like an automated spell check tool, grammar check is excellent for a first round of proofreading and editing. It can draw your attention to obvious errors that need to be adjusted, and get you thinking about what other errors may be lurking beyond grammar checker's scope. However, like spell check, you cannot just mindlessly click "accept" and "ignore." Sometimes fiction writers have a good reason for making a sentence grammatically incorrect. Style is important, and part of your work as a self-editor is to keep your tone and style consistent. And, of course, it bears repeating - grammar checker will not catch everything! You will have to go back through your work, sentence by sentence, to make sure each one is clear. Don't trust the programs!

FIND AND REPLACE

While it takes a bit more effort than the spelling and grammar check, find and replace is an effective tool for cleaning up your manuscript. Are there words you commonly misuse? Are you a serial offender of using *you're* when *your* is the correct choice? Get yourself to the find and replace tool. Type in the word you commonly misspell or misuse, and go through each occurrence of it meticulously. You can also use the find tool to ensure that you avoid falling into repetitive or unnecessary word usage traps. Do you know that you have a problem with overusing the word *very*? If so, search for that word in the find tool and think of a better way to write the sentences in which the offending word appears. Another trick for using the find tool to edit is particularly helpful for fiction writers. If you're writing fiction and have made up complicated names for people and places, it's likely you've transposed some letters in those unfamiliar words. If you find you've misspelled a character's name once, it's likely you've done it a few times. Type the misspelled version into the find window, the correct version into the replace window, and voila! Trust the programs this time.

GRAMMARLY

As Grammarly advertises on their homepage, it has a feature that regular spell check does not: "Grammarly spots erroneous use of lose/loose, affect/effect, lie/lay, there/their/they're, and many other commonly confused words." The browser extension and copy and paste functions are free to use, but accessing all of the program's features will require a premium subscription. If you write for a living, a premium subscription could be a valuable investment as you can use it for every blog post, article, and essay you write. You might also just consider the time you can save by using Grammarly to be worth the investment. But don't think that paying for a premium Grammarly subscription means you're going to get away with not reading and proofreading your manuscript yourself. There is no avoiding that.

In addition to its browser extension mode, Grammarly can be used as an add-in for Microsoft Word. The program's flexibility makes it an effective tool, but again, comes with the warning that no software will ever be as effective as a well-trained human for editing.

Purdue OWL

The OWL, which stands for Online Writing Lab, is a treasure trove of information for writers. It is free, it is searchable, and it is valuable for fiction and nonfiction writers alike. Hosted by Purdue University, you can access the resource at www.owl.english.purdue.edu. Once there, you can refresh your memory about everything from parts of speech to dan-gling modifiers to sentence fragments. Perhaps the most useful aspect of the OWL, though, is the information it houses about proper citation. The OWL has manuals availa-ble on the MLA, Chicago, APA, and AMA style guides, all available for you to use. Nonfiction writers who have a quick question about their citations, or who want to clarify some-thing that is in their chosen style guide, will find the OWL to be generally user-friendly and a good resource during the writing and editing phases of a project. If you like this web-site, it will be worth bookmarking, as you will find yourself continuously returning to it for guidance.

Scrivener

Available for both Mac and Windows, Scrivener is writing software with a bevy of features that help with the entire writing process, not just editing. The program has the typical spelling and grammar check programs, but it is especially effective for developmental editing. With Scrivener, you'll also have easy access to your notes and outlines, making it easier to move entire chapters around than in a typical word processing program.

Electronic resources make initial editing much more efficient, but, in case you didn't get the message the first few times: nothing replaces a human brain that understands the context and style needs of a work, and that knows the distinction of words like *your* and *you're*. Make sure you're not relying solely on programs.

HEMINGWAY APP

Named after the master of concise prose, this app can help you cut down on long-winded sentences that only add clutter to your writing. The app informs you if you've used too many adverbs, if the passive voice is stunting your message, and how many of your sentences are "hard to read" or "very hard to read." You can cut and paste portions of your writing into the website, www.hemingwayapp.com, or download it for use as a desktop app on a Mac or PC for a nominal fee. Even if you don't run your entire work through the program, just using it for a couple paragraphs every now and then can alert you to common errors. If you think you are a concise writer, the Hemingway App will probably change your mind and result in improved writing.

CONSISTENCY CHECKER

Consistency Checker is an add-on that can be used in Microsoft Word or Google Docs. The program doesn't check for spelling or grammatical errors, but as its name indicates, keeps you on the straight and narrow when it comes to style consistency. As we previously mentioned, sticking with one style can really make the difference when it comes to people considering your work to be professional. Whether you're working with the *AP Style Guide* or *The Chicago Manual of Style*, it is crucial to remain consistent. With Consistency Checker you can see where you've used hyphens in one place but not another, where you've spelled out numbers in some places and used numerals in others, and how you've altered an abbreviation from one chapter to another. Some of these errors can be found using the Find feature in Word, but Consistency Checker allows you to go much deeper. Plus, it's more automated so you won't have to manually type in every word or phrase you think might be inconsistent throughout your writing.

None of these resources on their own will provide all of the answers you are looking for, and it is always possible they may contradict each other. This is especially true in the case of style guides. Do not go looking for answers in both of these. Choose one, and stick with it. We cannot emphasize this enough. You also might simply find some of the resources to be more of a nuisance than a help. If your writing style is never going to be terse, or one of your characters always speaks in long, winding sentences, then the Hemingway App is going to cause more problems than it solves. Test out a few of the resources, see what works for you, and use those. Your writing style is unique, and it is what sets your voice apart. You also will have your own working habits that make some resources better for you than others. If you proofread on a printed copy and are easily distracted by the computer, then it doesn't make sense for you to rely on the Purdue OWL to answer your questions. Instead, keep *The Elements of Style* or *Grammar Girl* close as you edit. Only you know how you work best, so trust yourself and use the resources that fit your needs.

COMMON ERRORS TO LOOK FOR

It can be daunting and uninspiring to go back to the beginning of a work you've spent a significant amount of time on already. But if you know what to look for, it can make the self-editing process much smoother. There are some common errors that all writers are going to make, no matter how many books they've written, or how many times they've read *The Elements of Style*. That's because writers are human and the hands and fingers that use the keyboards and pens are going to screw up at some point. Not to mention, the English language can be a tad complicated at times.

Let's start with the basics—bad grammar. A reader will be distracted if your work has scattered grammatical errors. When you are typing quickly, in the heat of the excitement about your story, it is easy to misuse words like affect/effect, then/than, who/ whom, your/you're, and the dozens of others that English makes so easy to screw up even if you are a grammar fiend. You should also look for errors in spacing—a lot is not a word! And *into* and *in to* have distinct meanings.

Then there's *further* and *farther*, *can* and *may*, *less* and *fewer*, and *lay* and *lie*. That's just the beginning of the list of words that are easy to misuse. The references listed earlier are excellent resources for determining the proper usage of such words, and we've included some of them below for quick reference.

Accept *Except*	To receive; to agree Not included	I accept your apology. I like all vegetables except corn.
Advice *Advise*	Recommendation about what to do To recommend something; provide guidance	I need advice from a professional. I would advise you to wear a seatbelt.
Affect	To change or make a difference to	This humidity affects my hair.

Effect	The result of something	Being tired has an effect on my mood.
All together *Altogether*	All in one place; all at once Completely	The children gathered all together. He is altogether irritated!
Allusion *Illusion*	An indirect reference to something Misleading appearance or vision	That song is an allusion to his ex-wife That ghost is just an illusion.
Assure *Ensure* *Insure*	To promise that something is true To guarantee or make sure of something To take out an insurance policy	I assure you that I'll pick you up later. Sunscreen ensures you won't burn. You should insure your new car.
Bare *Bear*	Naked; to uncover To carry; to tolerate	That baby had a bare bottom. I cannot bear this heat any longer!
Brake *Break*	To stop a vehicle, a device that stops a vehicle To stop or pause; to separate into pieces	Keep your foot on the brake. I am ready for my lunch break.

Complement / *Compliment*	To make complete; bring to perfection / Praise; to say something nice	That rug complements the curtains. I got a compliment about my new dress.
Farther / *Further*	Used when talking about physical distance / Used when talking about figurative distance	I don't think I can run any farther. Don't read any further in the book.
Loose / *Lose*	To unfasten; not contained / To misplace	The rabid fox is on the loose! Why do I always lose my keys?
Principal / *Principle*	The head of a school; presiding officer; a sum of money lent / A belief system	You better go to the principal's office. Telling lies goes against my principles.
Sight / *Site*	The ability to see / A location	That paining is such a pretty sight. I can't wait to get to our tent site.
Stationary / *Stationery*	Unmoving / Writing materials	The parked car was stationary. I use fancy stationery to write letters.
Than / *Then*	Used when comparing something / At that time; next in order	I'd rather walk than run. We'll go to lunch and then get dessert.

Just as it is easy to misuse words when you're typing fast, it's also easy to misuse punctuation. You might find that you've put periods where a sentence shouldn't end, or that your comma usage is way out of whack. Commas are particularly easy to misuse when you're writing, especially if you have a tendency for big ideas that you cram into long sentences. Now, we're not going to start up a debate over the Oxford comma in this book, but whether you're an Oxford comma devotee or a hater, the most important thing is to keep your usage (or lack thereof) consistent throughout your work. In case you aren't familiar with the Oxford comma, we'll explain it here and then you can decide if you think it should be used in your work. For what it is worth, we are diehard Oxford comma devotees. An Oxford comma, also known as a "serial comma" is the last comma in a list. It always goes before the final word in a list and "and." Here are some examples.

With the Oxford comma: *My heroes are my parents, the Pope, and Mother Theresa.*

Without the Oxford comma: *My heroes are my parents, the Pope and Mother Theresa.*

Spot the discreet, yet important difference? In the first example, it is obvious that this person's heroes are his parents, AND the Pope, AND Mother Theresa. The second example is written in such a way that it is appears his parents ARE the Pope and Mother Theresa, who also happen to be his heroes.

Here's another example:

I'm having my favorite sandwich, pickles, and chocolate cake.

OR

I'm having my favorite sandwich, pickles and chocolate cake.

It's doubtful that anyone's favorite sandwich is pickles and chocolate cake, but that is exactly how the sentence reads without the Oxford comma. When it is in place, it's obvious that the person is eating his favorite sandwich as well as some pickles and a piece of cake.

Our bias shows through in our description, but technically, the Oxford comma is optional in American English. And there are instances when the use of an Oxford comma, even in a list, doesn't change the meaning. However, when it is needed, it is REALLY needed. Time and time again, there have been examples of when omitting the Oxford comma can lead to confusion, or even be the basis for a lawsuit! In 2017, a Maine-based dairy company lost millions of dollars in a dispute about overtime rules for its employees, simply due to the interpretation of state law that did not include an Oxford comma when there should have been one in place. This brief excerpt from a *Boston Globe* article on March 16, 2017 highlights how a simple omission caused a great deal of havoc for this business.

"The debate over commas is often a pretty inconsequential one, but it was anything but for the truck drivers. Note the lack of Oxford comma — also known as the serial comma — in the following state law, which says overtime rules do not apply to:

'The canning, processing, preserving, freezing, drying, marketing, storing, packing for shipment or distribution of:

(1) Agricultural produce;

(2) Meat and fish products; and

(3) Perishable foods.'

Does the law intend to exempt the distribution of the three categories that follow, or does it mean to exempt *packing for* the shipping or distribution of them?

Delivery drivers distribute perishable foods, but they don't pack the boxes themselves. Whether the drivers were subject to a law that had denied them thousands of dollars a year depended entirely on how the sentence was read.

If there were a comma after "shipment," it might have been clear that the law exempted the distribution of perishable foods. But the appeals court on Monday sided with the drivers, saying the absence of a comma produced enough uncertainty to rule in their favor. It reversed a lower court decision.

In other words: Oxford comma defenders won this round."

Right now, you might be thinking, "Sure, I can mess up commas, but how could I mess up a period?" A period is one of the simplest punctuation marks to use properly, but it is possible you've slipped up and let phrases through where full sentences should be. If you're writing fiction, you will understandably have style needs that require you to break grammatical rules now and then. If you're trying to establish a fast-paced scene or have authentic dialogue, then you will probably be writing some phrases set off with periods. That's okay. Just make sure that you aren't writing phrases in error, and that full sentences exist where they are needed. Also be sure that you have periods where they are needed. Run-on sentences can throw off the pacing of your writing and confuse a reader. If a reader has to go back to the beginning of a sentence and re-read it to figure out what it means, or because they've forgotten how the sentence started, then it's probably a run-on sentence. In this case, you need to rewrite, or break it up into two separate sentences.

Question marks and exclamation points are in a similar vein to periods. Pretty simple to use correctly, right? Well, exclamation points are a bit more subjective than question marks, but it never hurts to make sure you're not overusing them. Do you have a dialogue where the same character uses an exclamation point more than once on the same page? Unless you're aiming for campy, you probably want to remove some of those exclamation points. And never use more than one exclamation point to end a sentence!

It never hurts to double-check the question marks, either. You might have started out writing an interrogative sentence, but edited it as you were writing, and your brain just forgot how you decided to end the sentence. Pay attention to all of the punctuation marks in your work, no matter how simplistic you believe they are.

Slightly more complicated are colons and semicolons. This is where your style guides and grammar resources will become invaluable. While most writers are familiar with the basic rules guiding the use of these punctuation marks, most writers will also have questions at some point. As mentioned before, English is complicated, and that goes for punctuation requirements as much as it does the words themselves. When you are editing your work and you come across a colon or semicolon that you threw in there while furiously typing, take the thirty seconds to open your preferred grammar guide and double check your usage. Even if the punctuation mark is used correctly, checking on the usage will make you stop, think, and possibly even notice a way to improve the sentence's construction. Also, the more you check these marks the more intuitive your understanding of their usage (and your propensity for certain mistakes) will become. As a result, you will be able to edit faster and more accurately. Some common errors in the usage of colons, semicolons, and dashes include:

- Using a semicolon to introduce a list instead of a colon

- Using a semicolon where a comma would be more appropriate
- Using a semicolon to set off items in a list without internal punctuation
- Using a colon to introduce dialogue when a comma will do

Some quick tips when editing for proper use of semi-colons, colons, and dashes are included below for your reference.

The two main reasons to use semi-colons are to help separate items in a list when some of those words contain commas. Another reason is to join two sentences, using the punctuation mark between two independent clauses.

When using for listing purposes: *I bought shiny, firm apples; juicy, plump strawberries; and sweet, crunchy granola.*

Joining two sentences: *I went to the market. I bought fruit and granola for our snack.* While these sentences can stand fine on their own, they can also be combined into one: *I went to the market; I bought fruit and granola for our snack.*

In addition to the obvious use of colons for time (4:45), and in greetings (*To Whom it May Concern*), it has two other purposes.

- To introduce a list, a noun or noun phrase, a quotation, or an example.

My best friend gives me everything I need: a listening ear, good advice, and loyalty.

- To join sentences. This can be done to two consecutive, related sentences (complete independent clauses) when the second sentence explains, sharpens, or summarizes the first.

A whale is not a fish: it is a warm-blooded mammal.

Colons are also used when introducing a quote.

Hamlet asked one of life's greatest questions: to be or not to be.

Colons are often used incorrectly, and we recommend utilizing one of the reference books mentioned in this book to gain a better understanding of correct and incorrect uses. These examples are only a sampling. A good question to ask yourself when pondering the use of a colon is whether the material before the colon can stand on its own. If the words before the colon do not form a complete thought, you're likely using the colon incorrectly.

Dashes are a punctuation mark that can easily be overused, and when that is the case, they can interrupt the flow of your writing, resulting in choppier prose. One rule of thumb is to think of the dash as the opposite of a parenthesis. Dashes serve to emphasize the material (parenthesis, not so much). For example: *After having it on her bucket list for her entire life, the aging woman finally decided to make the trip she had always dreamed of—going to France.*

Dashes can also be used for introductions or conclusions to a sentence. *To maintain a healthy lifestyle, most adults need to do many things—eat balanced meals, exercise, and focus on stress reduction.*

In a sentence that already contains commas, a dash can be helpful when adding a phrase that further strengthens the sentence. For example: *All of my favorite hobbies—reading, writing, and running—require more free time than I currently have.*

Lastly, another common use of the dash is to break up dialogue, whether to depict an interruption or someone who might be stumbling over their words. Check your reference books to learn more about the proper use of dashes, especially when trying to determine whether a comma would be a better use.

Quotation marks are another form of punctuation that you need to keep an eye on. We all know that quotation marks are used to indicate dialogue, but in the modern era, quotation marks have fallen victim to the trend of indicating emphasis with words other than dialogue. This is not okay. When quotation marks are used outside of dialogue, they are widely considered to indicate sarcasm. If you find that you have tried to emphasize a point through the use of quotation marks, you need to rewrite the sentence. Your writing will absolutely be stronger for having done so, and you will avoid the embarrassing predicament of a reader assuming you were trying to indicate sarcasm when that was not your intent.

Another common error to look out for with the use of quotation marks is the placement of other punctuation outside of the marks.

Incorrect: "What are you talking about"? said the author.

Correct: "This is what I mean," said the editor.

Of course, this is true only in American English. If you're wondering why you see punctuation outside the quotation marks on occasion, that's because our British friends across the pond allow for the placement of punctuation outside of quotation marks. Ultimately, when you have questions about what to do and where to put punctuation when you use quotation marks, your chosen style guide is your best friend. Again, direction may differ between guides; the important thing is to just stay consistent with your chosen guide.

While self-editing, you should also look for common errors that are less technical than grammar and punctuation mistakes, but are nonetheless detrimental to the strength of your work. One such common error is the use of the passive voice. As its name suggests, the passive voice weakens your writing by taking the action out of it. Consider these sentence pairs:

The man was eaten by a grizzly bear.
The grizzly bear ate the man.

The treasure was found by the pirate.
The pirate found the treasure.

Which of each pair is not only more exciting, but clearer? That would be the second example in each pair, both of which are written in the active voice. When you use the passive voice you often have to use more words to say the same thing. Doing so drags out and complicates your point while weakening any kind of drama or excitement. There's a reason the passive voice is often used by politicians - it allows for a point to be clouded without it being a falsehood. A September, 2016 *Washington Post* article by Barton Swaim titled "'The system is rigged': How politicians use the passive voice as a rhetorical cheat" delves into this phenomenon, with Swaim citing the oft-used political phrase "mistakes were made" to illustrate his point. No one gets blamed for the mistake with the passive voice, and the politician still gets to sound like they are sorry for something. Do you want your writing to sound like you are hedging around a point, or do you want to make your story and your characters clear, strong, and engaging?

It is easy to slip into the passive voice when you are writing, especially if you are still unclear about where a plot is headed or how a certain character is developing. This is why it is so important to look for during the editing process. By the time you are editing for errors like the passive voice, you will be so familiar with your story that turning passive sentences into active ones will be a relatively painless process. It will also make your writing much stronger. The next time you sit down to pen even so much as a blog post you will find yourself writing in the active voice more naturally. And when you don't write in the active voice, you will notice it more quickly.

This isn't to say the passive voice is always wrong. In some instances it is necessary. Be attuned to the style needs of your work, but use the active voice as often as you can.

Another common error that is not technically wrong, but is a weak way to write, is the overuse of certain words. Some of the worst offenders include *really*, *just*, *very*, and *actually*. You can search for these words using the Find tool in your writing software. As each occurrence appears, consider how you might rewrite the sentence to make it stronger without that word. In many cases, you might find that the meaning of the sentence isn't affected at all by deleting the offending word. Let's compare a couple of sentences:

The ice cream is really good.
The ice cream is delicious.

I'm having a really hard time.
I'm struggling.

The fish was very smelly.
The fish was putrid.

When you see those sentences next to each other, it becomes clear that the extraneous adverbs and adjectives are diminishing the sentence's power. Want someone to have a gross image of rotting fish in their head? Using *putrid* will accomplish that in a way *very smelly* simply cannot.

In addition to the words mentioned above, you are probably aware of the words you have a bad habit of overusing. Search for those. You will surprise yourself with how many unnecessary words are scattered throughout your writ-ing. Remove them and your writing will be tighter, more engaging, better.

PART TWO: THE EDITING PROCESS

So now you're ready to go through your manuscript. Don't just dive in, however. There's an approach we recommend.

STEP ONE: TAKE A BREAK

Put it away. That's right—don't even think about starting to edit your manuscript right now. You've been focused on writing for months, possibly even years, and you're wrapped up in your story and your characters. You could probably recite some of the passages you've written by heart, and you've probably had dreams about your book. So why is that bad? You're too close to your work. If you're close to your work, you're more apt to miss mistakes. Or, you'll see developmental errors but be able to gloss over them with your own knowledge of how the plot is supposed to work. However, your future readers won't have that knowledge. So put your work down.

Then, for a least a week, don't return to your work. Yes, a full week. While you've been away from your manuscript, your brain has probably been churning through some thoughts about your story. Maybe you've even mulled over possible plot holes or ways to strengthen certain scenes, and these thoughts will be fresh in your mind when you sit down to edit. By distancing yourself from the words you've written, you've given yourself and your brain the breathing space needed to separate your writing brain from your editing brain.

You're always going to be close to your work, but time away from it removes some of the danger associated with self-editing. By giving yourself time to think critically about your work, you'll have fresher eyes and a fresher mind when you sit back down to begin the editing process. This will make it easier for you to catch everything from glaring plot holes to missing conjunctions. As a result, the editing process will go more smoothly and your final product will be cleaner and stronger.

Your work doesn't have to sit while you take your break, however. If you have someone you trust, now is a good time to provide them with a first draft. Be sure to let them know it is a rough draft, but that you'd appreciate honest input on the overall story, as well as any plot holes or scenes they think could be made stronger. At this point, unless they notice glaring typos like a name spelled several different ways throughout the work, don't have them spend a lot of time nitpicking for errors. You might be rewriting entire paragraphs, making that level of proofreading work premature.

However, while your friend or family member is looking through your rough draft, do not talk to them about it until your week is up. This is part of your quarantine. Stay away from your manuscript. You can do it, and it will be worth it. When your week is up, head back to your computer. Your eyes will be fresh and your brain will be ready to tackle the editing job.

STEP TWO: LISTEN TO YOUR BOOK

Your week of separation is over and your fingers are itching to start clicking away at the mouse. Once again, we're going to tell you to stop. Don't jump into it just yet. Self-editing takes discipline, and should be done methodically in order to prevent you from skipping over errors or glossing over weak spots just because you already know the story. The week that you spent away from your work helped to distance you from it and give you a mental break, but it didn't completely erase the story from your brain or cut your psychological ties to what you've written. So that means you need to take another step to put some distance between you and what you've written. The difference this time? You will be working with the manuscript and jotting down notes and thoughts about what you need to change. How do you do this? You listen to the manuscript.

Yes, the words are still the same. Why does listening make a difference? It's a new way of interacting with the manuscript. When you were writing, you were seeing your story on the page. You were working with it on the computer screen and likely only repeating the words to yourself silently in your head, if at all. When you do that, your brain will correct missing words, so if you are reading quickly you will fill in the word rather than notice it is not there! Think about the brainteasers you see sometimes on the internet, the ones that say "Can you find mistake?" or something similar, and the mistake is that the word *the* is missing, or *the* is written twice. Many people take quite some time to figure that out because of the very phenomenon that will cause you to overlook missing words in your own writing.

Have you ever read and reread an important email only to discover after you sent it that you spelled *the* as *hte* and didn't notice it at all? That's what you're trying to avoid by reading out loud.

When you're reading out loud, you are forced to go more slowly and be deliberate. You can't skim across the page with your eyes, not really taking in what is there. If you did, you wouldn't be able to comprehend enough to say the words out loud. That's how reading your work out loud becomes an effective tool for finding errors.

Reading aloud can also help you pinpoint sections of your writing that can be improved by working on the rhythm of the writing. When you read a sentence aloud, you might hear a poetic beat to it that works or doesn't work with the rest of your writing style. You might be stricken with an idea about how a two-syllable word would work better in a sentence than a three-syllable word, or how a short sentence followed by two longer sentences really throws off the pace of the action sequence you are trying to establish. In The *Elements of Style*, Strunk & White discuss how crucial it is to the success of The Gettysburg Address that Lincoln recognized the efficacy of the cadence of "Four score and seven years ago…" as opposed to "In 1776…" Take a beat and think about the difference in those two phrases, and if the latter would have remained ingrained in the American psyche for the last century and a half. Probably not. So listen to how your words sound out loud. Readers will be repeating them in their head as they read, and to build an effective rhythm or to wow them with the beauty of your prose, you need to know how the words and sentences work together and build on one another.

You don't have to be the one to read your work aloud, though. You just have to be able to listen to it. If you have a friend or family member who is willing to help you out, have them read it out loud while you listen. You could do a few pages a day, or meet on the weekend to sip coffee and work. Just make sure you are okay with their voice and the natural pace at which they will read to you. Remember how you used to cringe whenever certain kids would get called on to read aloud in class, even if they were one of your best friends? Some people just don't have a natural talent for reading out loud. If you're going to be listening to someone read your work, it's going to take a lot of time, and you need to be able to focus on the editing process while you listen. You also need to be able to make requests of the person, like telling them to speed up or slow down or not insert their own commentary between every single sentence. Letting someone else into your writing and editing process can be tough, but if you have the right person in mind and they are willing to help out, it will an enormous benefit.

Not comfortable having someone read your draft manuscript? Another option is to use a computer's text to speech function. By doing this you avoid any potential minefields from working with a friend or family member, you avoid having to read the manuscript aloud yourself, and you can mark up the manuscript as you work. Both Windows and Mac computers have text to speech functions that are relatively simple to use, and don't require any equipment other than a computer speakers.

On a Windows computer, it is a function called Narrator that you access either by using the Start button, or by pressing the Windows key + Enter in Windows 10. You will need to select the text you want read aloud after opening Narrator.

On a Mac system, navigate to System Preferences and from there to Dictation & Speech, then Text to Speech. You'll be given the option to choose which key combination you would like to use to have your computer read aloud selected text. Leave at default if you wish, or use the "Change Key" button to make it an easy combo for you to remember.

An even easier option on Mac, if you are working in Pages, is to select a portion of text, CTRL + click, hover over "speech," and select "start speaking." Voila! You will start hearing your words read back to you. Isn't technology great?

When you are using the text to speech function, only take on small portions of your manuscript at a time. Don't hit "select all" and just have it start reading. Listening to your work in manageable sections will make you work more deliberately. You'll also feel a sense of accomplishment every time you finish a segment, giving you the boost and motivation you need to keep going. The downside to this approach compared to having a friend read is that it's easier to tune out the computer. Having a friend read keeps you paying attention, and has the added benefit of your friend picking up errors.

If you don't like the Mac and Windows text to speech default programs, there are several others available that you can install and try. Among those you might want to try are:

- Ghost! Clipboard Reader (compatible with Windows)
- NaturalReader (compatible with Windows)
- Readthewords.com (online program)
- GhostReader (compatible with Mac)

Once you have figured out which program works for you, you need to decide how to go about the actual task of editing while you listen. There are two ways to do this. Some of us work better on printed paper, and others are able to work quite well directly on a screen. If you work better on printed paper, have a copy of your manuscript in front of you and make notes as you listen. Then, when you go into the computer to make changes, you have a copy to work from that you can save and refer back to if you have questions later in the editing process about what you've done.

If you are the kind of person who can work just as well on a screen as you can on the printed page, follow along with the text that's being read aloud and make changes directly onto your document. It is always a good idea to create a copy so that you have the original saved to for reference at a later date if necessary. Working directly on the computer rather than using a two-step process involving a printed copy is certainly faster, but depending on your reading and comprehension style, it may not be the most effective. Only you know the best way you work, so trust your instincts.

As you work, you might decide to try a new method. That's fine. Working with a friend or family member might become cumbersome after a chapter or two, or you might decide that when you're reading out loud to yourself you simply don't focus as well. Try a new method, download a new program, or find a new friend. Try all of the above it that works best. The important thing is that you are working in a way that allows you to focus on the words, the sentences, and the story itself so that your writing is the best it can be.

STEP THREE: CHECK FOR NARRATIVE AND CHARACTER ARC

If your book is nonfiction, you can skip to Step Four. If your book is fiction, and you want to pull readers in and keep their attention, this step is important. Your book has to make sense, which means that your book has to have a structure that allows the characters and story to develop in natural and logical way. The narrative and character arcs must also be interesting if you want to keep your audience's attention.

At the very least, you probably remember the discussions of static and dynamic characters from English classes. The static character, as the name implies, doesn't change from the beginning to end. The dynamic character does. There are the typical character arcs: change (a.k.a. hero), growth, and fall. Before starting your book, you had an idea of which of these character arcs your protagonist would follow, and likely how any other supporting characters would change throughout the book, and how the static characters support or inhibit the dynamic character's changes and the story's development on the whole. During the writing process, however, it is likely that you came up with new ideas and creative dialogue for your characters. That's natural! It's part of the fun of the writing and part of the creative process. Sometimes, though, it's possible that snippets of dialogue or descriptions of action simply don't fit with your character's personality and their overall arc throughout the story. Such discrepancies can throw off your reader, and in doing so make your character less relatable and the story less consistent.

At this point, you have written your book, probably outlined it, and listened to it read aloud at least once. You have spent literally hundreds of hours getting to know these characters. No one knows them and their quirks and backstories better than you do. However, that does not mean that you can just insert an obvious deviation that detracts from their character arc without explaining it in the book. Just because you, as the author, know why the character did something does not mean it is clear to the reader. Likewise, you cannot have characters who just show up randomly for the sake of showing up. They detract from the story. Everything in your book should move the plot along in some way, in a *believable* way that makes sense within the world you've created.

As you are editing, make a note where you think your character might be saying or doing something that isn't within their personality or that doesn't necessarily fit within the story. This will help you keep those details in mind as you continue working, and you might realize that what you made a note of does fit with plot movement later on in the book. Just be careful you're not forcing something to fit, though.

Like a character arc, your story arc needs to make sense. As we all learned in elementary school, your story should have a beginning, middle, and end. This is the most basic form of a story arc, and as you are editing you should be able to tell which portion of the story you are in. If you can't, it's quite possible significant developmental editing is needed. But don't despair! Sometimes, you can move an entire chapter around without much pain, editing only the beginning and ending sentences. Paying close attention to how your story progresses, and how each scene builds the action or gives necessary information to the reader is crucial to having a strong, compelling work.

Another thing to consider for your character and story arcs is how much information is too much information. You probably have a deeply developed idea of what happened to the characters in your book before they began the adventure you are putting down on paper. They all had childhoods, wacky relatives, bad experiences, and good experiences that made them into the person they are when they first appear on paper. However, does every detail about their past or about their physical appearance matter to their role in your story and to the story overall? Does the fact that the town in your story was founded in 1654 matter to the plot? These kinds of details do impact your plot and character development. If they aren't necessary, they are nothing but a distraction and a way to bore or confuse the reader. As you decide what matters to your plot and character development, you can always keep Elmore Leonard's, a successful American novelist, strategy in mind while you're writing and editing to help guide you: "I try to leave out the parts that people skip."

Long descriptions about your character's past might be fascinating to you, but if they add nothing to the story, your reader won't be entertained or enlightened and you'll just have more details to contend with that could be throwing off your plot.

Some of the details you choose to include in your story, whether details about action or details about objects or characters, might be included in order to foreshadow future events. As you're reading to see how your story progresses, consider just how much these details actually give away. Readers don't want to know from page two that a specific character is going to die because you mentioned an arsenic bottle next to their teacup thinking you were being sly, but if you can finesse foreshadowing in such a way that it doesn't give too much away, it can be effective tactic for capturing the reader's attention. Perhaps mentioning that arsenic bottle *does* make sense to the story. Only you (and your beta readers) will know. The best foreshadowing lets the reader know that they should probably pay attention to a character, object, or bit of dialogue without knowing exactly why. Or, it should stick in their mind so when action happens later in the story, the reader can think back and go "Oh! That's what that meant!" There is a big difference between that happening, and a reader figuring out the entire plot in the second chapter because you slipped in details or action that should not have been included, or should have been written into the story later. Just because you know what is going to happen throughout the entire book doesn't mean your reader is going to. And you absolutely do not want them to. They need to have a reason to keep reading, and suspense is a major motivator. Check your story arc not only for unnecessary details, but harmful details.

If you did not work from an outline while writing, it is more likely that you will have issues with your story arc that need to be addressed. Everyone has their own writing method, and some people prefer to put the time into creating a detailed outline, while others prefer to put the time into heavy developmental editing once the words are on paper. You know how you work best, so where you put your time is up to you.

It is perhaps obvious advice that your story arc needs to make sense, but sometimes it is very easy to get off on a tangent when writing, resulting in a section—or entire chapter—that doesn't add anything to, or possibly detracts from, the story. Maybe it is necessary information for moving the plot along, but it's just in the wrong place. Don't be afraid to cut and paste entire paragraphs when editing.

Editing story and character arcs isn't all about deletion, though. It's important to recognize when you need to add in a detail or a paragraph in order to complete the picture. When you go through your work with this in mind, it will become clearer to you if an element is coming out of nowhere and needs a better buildup.

Editing a story's different arcs might seem like a daunting task, especially if you didn't start out writing from an outline. One way to make the job a bit more manageable is to create an outline as you go. Read a chapter, then mark down its overarching role in the action in a sentence or two. Under that, note in a sentence or so what each character's action or contribution toward plot movement is in that chapter. As you do this, you'll be able to see what elements are missing, what might need to be moved around, or what can be edited out altogether. By outlining what you have actually written, you'll be forcing yourself to focus on the plot development and character development as it exists in the written word, and not as you envision it in your mind, or as you had fleshed it out in your pre-writing outline.

If you did create an outline before you began writing, another option is to take that outline and make notes on it as you are doing your plot and character arc edits. This way you can see how you might have deviated from the outline (which isn't necessarily a bad thing) and clean up and rearrange as needed to ensure your story is moving along nicely.

It might seem very obvious, but a successful story arc is only possible if your story begins well and ends well. Do you need that prologue and epilogue, or should you just jump right into the story and wrap it up with the last line of the book?

Consider whether or not a prologue provides too much backstory for your plot or your character. Does it give away information that is necessary to pique the reader's interest and help them understand the action of the book, or is it simply a way for you to avoid the complicated work of weaving a backstory's details into the narrative? Prologues can work, and they can be effective, but do not write one just for the sake of it, or because your favorite 19th century author always included one. Even if you don't have a prologue, look at the beginning of your book with a critical eye. Does it set up the plot and character arcs well? Do you start much further back in the story than is necessary, or do you start right where the reader needs to jump in to understand the characters' motivations and the plot's movement? These are all good questions to ask yourself. They are also good questions to ask anyone else who you have asked to read the book.

The beginning of your book should set up the action. If your first chapter is made up of description, with no hint of action or conflict, your reader is going to get bored from the outset. If they proceed to the second chapter, you then be in the position of trying to bring their interest back. You don't want to be in this position. If you don't capture the reader in the first chapter, you've likely already lost them. You've also wasted a lot of time and words setting up a story that you probably could have dived right into. That's not to say you need to delete your descriptive first chapter altogether, just consider how it might be revised or reworked to become significant. If you can't do that, perhaps you do need to remove it and see if you can weave some of the description into the story itself. You likely had a reason for including that description or background details in the first place, so don't dismiss it right off. But you need to know how it works with the rest of your plot. The beginning of your book is critical to your book's success, and it should get the plot off to a strong start.

You also need to look at which story threads you started your book with, and which of those threads you wrapped up in your conclusion. Nearly every book is going to have at least one subplot, and if you don't resolve that subplot in some way, your readers are going to be disappointed at best, and confused at worst. If you realize that you haven't wrapped up a subplot in your resolution, you might want to consider whether it is necessary for that story arc at all. Some subplots may be concluded around the middle of the book, driving the larger plot further overall, and that's a good thing. By the end of your book, though, there should not be any threads left untied, unless of course you are planning a series and you set up those threads to continue in the next book. That tactic is, in its own way, a conclusion for those subplots.

If you're looking for some creative inspiration and a useful, albeit somewhat basic, guide to story arcs, Kurt Vonnegut's descriptions might help kick-start your story arc editing process. A quick Google search of "Kurt Vonnegut's story arcs" or "Kurt Vonnegut's story shapes" will bring you to several examples, some complete with diagrams, of the basic story arcs as delineated by Vonnegut. Seeing these will help you identify the arc you intend for your novel, and then use them to compare your work. You can also use these arcs as a guide when creating your outline from the outset.

Editing for a story's various arcs can be difficult, and is certainly time-consuming, but using a few tools and tricks can make the process more effective. This is a part of the editing process where bringing in a second set of eyes or a second brain might prove most useful. A family member or friend won't know how your story is going to end, so they'll be able to pick out plot holes or obvious, clumsy foreshadowing where you might not see it. If you are depending on yourself for this editing, you can do it, but you need to separate yourself from the original story you've written and get into an objective mindset. If you find yourself slipping back into the author mindset, step away from your work and reset your brain. Read or watch something that has a different tone or is in a different genre from your book. Then, refocus on your objective mindset, and get back to editing the plot and character development. You had the focus to write the story, so you will have the focus to edit it. It just takes a bit of effort to get into the right mindset to do so.

STEP FOUR: CHECK CONSISTENCY

You need to make sure that your writing stays consistent throughout your manuscript. You can do this by re-reading just for consistency, or by keeping an eye out for issues as you are working on the story arc. You can also edit for elements of consistency while you are proofreading, but it is worth separating the two into distinct steps because you may find it easier to focus on different aspects of your work at a time.

So, what is editing for consistency? Editing for consistency is ensuring that your style stays the same throughout your writing. It also means checking on how you refer to things like people's names, places, etc. Does one character get called primarily by their last name for the first five chapters, but all of a sudden everyone is calling him by his first name in the sixth chapter? That's just going to confuse people. It can be difficult to edit for consistency because there is a lot to keep track of, particularly if your work is long. However, there are a few ways to make it easier.

First, don't wait to decide on a style guide. If you didn't pick one before you started writing, decide on one before you start editing. Generally, unless you're writing a journalistic nonfiction book, you'll be going with the *Chicago Manual of Style*. But whatever you do, don't start editing, get halfway through the book and have to start all over because you can't remember if you should be using the Oxford comma or not. That's a waste of your time, and a good way to get so frustrated you are tempted to give up on editing altogether. Self-editing is hard enough, so don't make it harder by neglecting simple tasks like selecting a style guide before you start.

Second, make a list of how names are used as you edit the first couple of chapters. Does Samantha Stevens go by

Samantha, Stevens, Sam, or Sammi? Does it change based on who is speaking to her? Does her mom call her one thing, but her best friend calls her another? By making a running list of such details (it doesn't have to be extensive—just enough so you understand and have a way to quickly check later on) you will have an easy resource when you reach later chapters, saving yourself from having to flip through pages at the beginning of your work. That is an unnecessary chore and will cost you a lot of time. Even editing on the computer and using the CTRL + F can be time-consuming if you are constantly doing it simply because you can't remember how a certain character was referred to early on in the book. It interrupts your workflow, whereas a simple glance at a list spurs your memory while keeping your place in the document for easier editing.

You can also use the list process for organizations, countries, or other phrases that might be turned into acronyms or abbreviations at some point. Do you say U.S. in some places but U.S.A. in others? These are the types of details that might seem inconsequential, but do make a difference in how professional your end product is. Larger details, like using names inconsistently can confuse a reader and, if bad enough, might frustrate them to the point they put the book down and leave a poor review.

In addition to names, abbreviations, or acronyms, there are several other things to look out for when editing for consistency. Many of them will be covered by the style guide you opt to use, so abide by the rules set out there. However, even knowing the rules doesn't ensure that you always follow them when you are writing in the heat of the moment. What matters at that point, when you're wearing your writer's hat, is the words themselves and staying in the flow of writing. In that moment, you don't care if a word should be capitalized. This is why you edit, and why you need to edit carefully, slowly, and deliberately.

So we've covered names and acronyms/ abbreviations, now let's look at what else to pay attention to when editing for consistency.

Hyphenation is one that trips up a lot of writers. Use your style guide as your primary reference for whether to hyphenate a phrase or not, but if you are unsure about a hyphen's proper usage in a particular phrase, just be sure that you keep that phrase consistent throughout your work. This is a situation where the find and replace tool can come in very handy. If you come across a phrase you are unsure of, or that you discovered you hyphenated (or did not hyphenate) erroneously even one time, it is worth doing a find and replace search. Chances are good that a phrase will appear only a few times throughout the work, making a find and replace absolutely worth the effort. Common areas to find missed hyphens are outlined below.

Numbers used in phrases

For example, *third-floor apartment* is correct, as is an *apartment on the third floor*.

Numbers used for ages is another. Three-year-old or 3-year-old or three year old? If you're using the *Chicago Manual of Style*, it's *a three-year-old*, but a toddler is *three years old*. And, if you're using AP Style, the hyphens are still there, but the numeric words become numerals. That's a topic for a different section, though.

Phrases with adverbs

Is it a much-needed nap or a much needed nap? A well-deserved break from editing or a well deserved break from editing? The hyphens belong there, but you might have missed putting one in when you were writing your first draft. As you go through your work, if you find that missing hyphens in phrases like this (adverb not ending in -ly, plus a participle or adjective - thank you, *Chicago*), the find and replace search could help. Do a search for "much" or "well" or "less" and evaluate the phrases in which you use those words.

Names

Do you call someone Mary-Beth in one chapter but

Mary Beth in the next? Well, hate to tell you, but you've really got to decide on which one to use. Names can present many problems with consistency and are especially important to pay attention to. Characters drive a story, and if your reader becomes confused by who you're talking about they're not connecting with the character or paying attention to the story's action.

We covered keeping the use of hyphens with numerical phrases consistent, but there are other ways in which numbers can affect your consistency. Namely, whether you spell them out or use the numerals. The *AP Style Guide* says numbers over ten should be spelled out, and that numbers used in ages should be numerals, not words (yup, we're at that section!).

When you're editing for consistency in numbers, you should also keep an eye out for how you are using commas. Of course, this will only matter if you are writing a work that includes big numbers, so it might be more of an issue for nonfiction writers. But if you're writing fiction, you still need to keep an eye out for inconsistencies. So is your main character running 1,245 miles to save his girlfriend or 1245 miles? When he doesn't find her is he crying 2,356 tears or 2356 tears?

Capitalization is another pitfall for consistency. While there are hard and fast rules for capitalization in English grammar, there are some instances where you might be making a decision to capitalize based on the message you want to send. The proper rules of English say you shouldn't capitalize *the general* in the sentence "I sent my report to the general," but if you are writing a story where the general is an intimidating, major figure, then you might have opted to always capitalize his title. If you did, then you should make sure you do so throughout the entire book. When it comes to capitalization, there are some consistent rules of thumb to follow, regardless of which style manual you utilize when editing. There are also many common mistakes people make when determining whether or not to capitalize.

When to Capitalize	
Example	
Brand Names and Companies	Nike, Whole Foods supermarket, Google
Governmental	Department of Commerce, the U.S. Constitution, Congress
Historical time periods	the Great Depression, the Spanish Civil War
Holidays	Fourth of July, Easter
Institutions	Yale University, Rhode Island School of Design
Landmarks	the Grand Canyon, the Statue of Liberty, Mount Rushmore
Manmade structures	the Eiffel Tower, the Great Wall of China
Organizations	the World Wildlife Fund, the American Civil Liberties Union
Planets (except for moon and sun)	Saturn, Mercury
Races, nationalities	Caucasian, African American
Religions, names of deities	Buddhism, Zeus, God, Christian
States, territories	Michigan, Dade County
Streets and roads	Main Street, U.S. Route 1

While some words are never capitalized, such as seasons, there are words that can be capitalized depending on their usage. An example would be when talking about the president. If you're referring to the president, unless you use it as a proper noun, such as President Obama or the President of the United States of America, you would not capitalize it. An example of this: *I am going to write a letter to the president.* Your best bet is to highlight any words that you question and then check your style guides for help. And always make sure you maintain consistency!

Consistency goes beyond checking individual words and phrases. It also coincides with developmental editing in that you need to ensure your characters stay consistent throughout the book. You need to make sure that their physical characteristics, background and biographical details, and personality traits all stay consistent. This doesn't mean making them boring, but it does mean that unless a deviation from their general personality is purposeful and an addition to the plot, it shouldn't happen. This is a lot easier if you have character sketches to work from, but as you read and re-read your work you will become so familiar with your characters that you will be able to tell what seems out of place. Also, when you are editing for consistency and you are reading a sentence that includes a biographical or physical detail about a character, stop reading. Take a breath, think through that detail, and consider if it matches up with what you have told the reader about the character already. If you are unsure or can't remember what you've already written in terms of background details about a character, it behooves you to use the find function, search for that character's name and quickly peruse other sentences that mention him or her. Likely, you will only need to do this if it's a minor character. But don't underestimate how much readers pay attention to minor characters—it is quite likely that a reader would pick up on the fact you called a character a teenager at the beginning of the story, but a few chapters later they are joining their siblings downtown for a beer without any mention of a fake ID or other step taken to procure underage entry into a bar.

Your characters' dialogue should also remain consistent. If you start out writing in a dialect for a character, maintain the use of that dialect. The way someone speaks is a part of their personality, and if you want to keep a character consistent and believable, you need to keep their speech patterns consistent and believable. Even if you are not creating a character with a certain dialect or accent, you should still pay attention to particular aspects of their speech. Something like whether or not they use contractions in their dialogue might seem trivial, but think about how you react when you hear someone speak in regular conversation without using contractions. Generally, if someone comes up to you and says, "Hello, I am John. I could not find my way to the store," you will immediately be struck by how formal they speak. Remember this when you are writing your character's dialogue and then again when you are editing it. It is easy to fall into the trap of writing with the use of contractions or without them, and fall into one pattern. When you are editing for consistency, though, you need to pay attention to how that pattern reflects on your characters. It's easy enough to spot contractions—look for an apostrophe in dialogue. Or, you can read aloud any dialogue you come across even when you are not in the reading aloud phase of editing. See if what you are hearing sounds like how you imagine your character to be speaking. Another option is to take the list of character names and use it to make notes about your characters' speaking habits. For example, you could note next to certain characters' names whether or not they speak in dialect, if they use contractions, if they are supposed to be educated or not, and refer to these notes while editing. You don't have to do this for every character, as you will know intuitively how your main characters speak, but if you are writing a book with many minor characters it can be a handy reference. Even a deviation in a minor character's speaking habits can affect their role in the story, so don't neglect any character as too minor for examination.

You must also edit for consistency in your characters' points of view. Is your main character speaking in first person to the reader, but then in another chapter the point of view changes to the third person without explanation? This is not only confusing to the reader, but it also throws off the plot. Some authors make a stylistic choice to switch between points of view for different characters or scenes, but if you do this it should have a purpose. It should illuminate something about your character, or help move the plot along. It should not be done just because you forgot which point of view you started out writing in, or because it was easier to craft a sentence in the first person point of view than in the third person point of view. It is easier to slip in and out of points of view than you may think, so be sure to keep that consideration in the back of your mind as you edit.

One of the most consistent issues we run across when editing for points of view is "head hopping," which occurs when the point of view changes from one character to the other while in the same scene or during a conversation. This can make it very confusing to readers and can really slow down the story's flow. There are two schools of thought on this, and some writers think head hopping is acceptable and allows for a more creative expression. In reality, however, it is rarely done well and is generally frowned upon. Regardless of what you choose or how you feel, you need to be consistent and make sure that there is not any unintentional head hopping. And, if you choose to allow for multiple points of view within the same scene, make sure it is very clear and does not create clunky prose.

Nonfiction books require checks for consistency that you likely will not need to make in a fiction book. If you're writing nonfiction, unless it is a memoir or first-person essay, it's likely you are going to be referencing other sources throughout the book. If you are, decide upon which style guide to abide by for citations and a bibliography before beginning. If you didn't, let's just say you've got your work cut out for you.

But let's start from the assumption you did opt for a style guide and were diligent about your citations throughout. There are still matters of consistency to look for, on top of proofreading your citations and bibliography. When you are checking your nonfiction work for consistency, how you use quotes should be top of mind. How are you using block quotes? Is it when a quote is more than three lines (check your style guide) or is it every quote? Are you using quotation marks around block quotes, a smaller font, or a different font? Every time you come across a quote in your writing, consider how it is formatted and how it is set apart from the rest of your writing. Is it set apart in the same way other quotes of its size are set apart? You may need to do a quick check after you finish the final formatting to confirm the number of lines in some quotes; if you change the margins, the length and number of lines may change and require you to add or subtract quotation marks and adjust the font. Keeping a cheat sheet nearby for quotes can help with this process. Even just an index card with a notation like "3+ lines = no quotes, Arial 11" or something to that effect can keep you on track. That way you don't have to highlight the quote, then go back and highlight the last quote, making sure the fonts match up and adjusting accordingly. Alternatively, if you are savvy with Word, you can use the Style options to set these in advance. Then you just have to highlight and click.

In your nonfiction work, and occasionally in fiction, you might use footnotes to add extra information on a page. When you do this, you have a few options of how to indicate the aside. You can use an asterisk, a number, or another symbol. Just make sure you are using the same symbols throughout. Don't use a number on one page, and then an asterisk on the next. Deciding what to use as an indicator of a footnote before you begin writing is the easiest way to ensure consistency, but if you did not, it is important to check footnote indicators. If you don't stay consistent with them, readers might wonder what is going on. They might think numbers mean they should flip to the back of the book, while asterisks direct them to the bottom of the page. They might just wonder in general what happened to the author's editor, thinking if they couldn't handle that level of detail, could the research really be accurate?

In the resources section, we mentioned the Consistency Checker program. Use the program to check for consistency, but as with any electronic tool, don't depend on it entirely. The program may be especially useful if you are the type of person who gets overwhelmed thinking about seemingly tiny details like hyphens, because it will at least get you started and point you toward what to look for. What the Consistency Checker program can't help you with is character and plot consistency. You're on your own there, but as you know your story and characters better than anyone, you are in the best position to check their consistency.

When editing for consistency, it's important that you come to a stopping point. As with editing overall, you're not going to catch everything. Do the best you can, but do not drive yourself crazy reading every page five or six times just hunting for hyphens. Be diligent, be detailed, but don't go overboard. Be sure to take breaks. Your brain gets tired, and when your brain gets tired it gets lazy and misses things. Work for an hour or so, then get up and stretch. Trying to edit an entire, full-length manuscript for something as detail-oriented as consistency isn't going to happen in one fell swoop. Give yourself time to take your breaks—your brain and your back will thank you.

Editing for consistency might sound like a lot of work, but once you get into the mindset of looking for certain words and phrases that are more likely to be used inconsistently, you will find yourself catching errors naturally as you work. Working slowly and deliberately might be frustrating, and it might seem unnecessary if you write carefully, but it will pay off in the end. Keep a running list, use Post-It notes in your chosen style guide, use your find and replace tool, or any other memory and organizational trick that you can think of. In the end, your writing will be cleaner, your reader will be less distracted, and your work will be more professional overall. If there's one thing we've been consistent with here, it's the importance of being consistent.

STEP FIVE: FACT-CHECK

Fact-checking? Yes, even with fiction. Just because you're writing fiction doesn't give you a free pass to have errors in your work.

When writing fiction, you want your reader to connect with the work and feel like they are a part of the world you have created. One way that a reader can become disconnected from a story is by noticing an inaccuracy. Inaccuracies separate the reader from the book by creating a sense of distrust in you, the author, as well as causing the reader to mull over the inaccuracy and the work it's associated with.

This reasoning surely makes sense if you are writing nonfiction and are asking a reader to trust that you are the authority on the subject. But it's also true when you're writing fiction. You are asking them to accept that you are the authority on the world and characters and story you've created. You're asking them to buy into the fact that this story is happening, whether in a real setting or a fictional world. If your story is set in a fictional world, like Tolkien's Middle Earth, then your fact-checking about that world might fall more in line with editing for consistency. However, if you set your story in New York City, you better be darn sure you check the facts about where landmarks are located, how long it takes to get from one place to another on the subway, and how big cockroaches can grow. Don't assume you know these things. Instead, take the time to double-check them. If you think a native New Yorker, or even an avid tourist, won't put down your book to send you an angry email, or write an angry review on their blog or, even worse, Amazon, you underestimate how much readers care about what they're reading.

You should also fact-check things like flowers and animals you mention. Are squirrels prevalent in southern cities? Double check this detail before you mention that your protagonist is always seeing them on the street in her neighborhood. Do they have weeping willows in France? Check that out before you have your character relaxing under one on a summer day. What grocery stores do they shop at in Florida? Hannaford, Aldi, or Publix? Of course, you can always entirely make a grocery store up, but that depends on how realistic or fantastic your story is, and how much of your imagination energy is left for naming grocery stores.

If you're basing your story in the real world, particularly in a geographic region you are familiar with, even vaguely so, you might think you are okay to skip the fact-checking all together. Don't. Especially if you have moved away from the area you are writing about. Things change in this world, and they change fast. That said, something you make reference to in your writing now might change in a few years, but that's not something you can control. Just do the best you can with the world you know, and the world you are writing in.

There is another level of fiction that requires stricter fact-checking—historical fiction. If you are writing historical fiction, you have purposely chosen to set your story in a time and place that you want to describe, that you want to tell the story of and bring to life. Yes, you are writing fictional characters (for the most part) and your story is mostly fictional, but the scene you are setting is not. Are your characters eating the foods they would at the time? Did the Tudors eat avocados? Would a girl in 1940s America have been allowed to wear jeans to school without causing a hullabaloo? I don't know, but if you're writing about the time period, you should! Presumably, if you're writing historical fiction you enjoy researching and have thoroughly researched the time period and place you are writing about. Just make sure to double check any details you might have overlooked during writing. Some things, like clothes and food, are just second nature to us and we don't consider how little details like that can derail a world.

The internet is right there at your fingertips, and fact-checking has never been easier than it is in this day and age. In addition to simply Googling the fact that you want to check and looking for authoritative websites, you can also use the internet to find your local library's website. Many libraries nowadays have live chat features or messaging/email services through which you can ask the reference librarian a question. Use this resource if you cannot find an answer while fact-checking. If they can't provide an outright answer, it's likely they will be able to provide a source or two that you can use, and, with your knowledge of your story's context, possibly find an answer in. If your local library doesn't provide such a service, head to Washington, D.C. Not physically of course, but virtually. The Library of Congress has an "Ask a Librarian" feature on their website, which has live chat options for certain subjects during certain times. With these kinds of resources at your fingertips, there is absolutely no reason you can't fact-check your writing.

Now, if you are writing nonfiction, the concept of fact-checking is going to be a much different beast than it is for a fictional story. Before you began writing you likely did an enormous amount of research, and you know your subject inside and out. You're writing and publishing on the topic because you are interested, in fact probably fascinated, by it. But that's not to say you can just write your work, edit for punctuation, and push it out to print. Your reputation hinges on the accuracy of your writing. When you are editing, double check dates, double check the attribution of quotes, and double check anything that makes you stop and go "hmm." Nonfiction writers are often at an advantage over fiction writers when it comes to fact-checking because of the copious amounts of research and painstakingly organized notecards or notebooks that you have close at hand. While fact-checking will still take time, just be glad you aren't starting from scratch when it comes time to check many of the details and assertions in your book. Making the effort to verify the assertions you are making is worth it in the long run. Sure, you might be delaying the printing of your book by a month, but that's better than only selling ten copies of your book because the reviews on its Amazon page are liberally sprinkled with words like "neophyte" and "sloppy." Don't risk it. Do the extra work. Go back through your notes when you need to. It's not a waste of time. Fact-checking is a crucial part of the editing process, and your book and your reputation deserve you making the effort.

STEP SIX: IMPROVE YOUR WRITING

If you've written a book, you must enjoy writing to some degree. And not only do you enjoy writing, but you are likely pretty good at it. You can probably string a sentence together more quickly and more eloquently than most of your friends and your vocabulary is probably fairly extensive. While you have a natural knack for the written word, that doesn't mean every sentence you craft is at its best on the first try. No, that doesn't mean punctuation is wrong, or you might have a misspelled word. It means entire words might need to be changed and entire sentences might need to be rearranged in order to make your writing the best it can be. There are four specific things to look for when editing to improve your writing: showing instead of telling, adverb overuse, concise language, and clichés.

When writing, you are trying to immerse a reader in a believable world. Even if you are writing nonfiction, you want the reader to be fully focused on your words. The best writers draw readers in by showing, not by telling. Even if you know this phrase (and surely, if you are writing for a hobby or profession you have heard it tossed around), it is easy to stray from the directive when you are writing your first draft. Early on in the writing process, the focus is usually on getting your ideas on paper before they fly away, trapping your inspiration on the page. While you may write well during this phase, it is during the editing phase that you can, and should, really polish your prose. So what do you look for when trying to determine whether your words show, and not tell?

First, character descriptions. Sometimes, you're just going to list physical characteristics, especially if you're writing a crime novel that requires suspect or victim descriptions. But when you're trying to elucidate the attractiveness of a character, even in the midst of a stormy crime scene, there are two ways to do that. Let's take a look:

Kristy was tall and blonde, and even in the middle of the rainstorm her beauty was enough that all of the men stopped paying attention to the corpse and locked their eyes on her.

That's okay, right? You know she's tall and blonde, you know they're all at a crime scene, outdoors, and it's raining. But how about this version?

Kristy's blonde hair whipped around her shoulders as the rain beat down around her. Thankfully, she didn't need heels to improve her height, and she was able to move swiftly in her flats across the muddy ground. She could sense the eyes of her male colleagues locked on her body, ignoring the dead one they were supposed to be examining, but she was used to their behavior by now.

In the second version, we learn that Kristy is tall and blonde, that it is raining out, that they are at a crime scene, and that her male colleagues are enthralled by her. But we also have an opportunity to learn a little bit more about her personality as we are drawn into the scene through her actions. Simply telling the reader "Kristy was tall and blonde" doesn't provide the opportunity for the reader to connect with the scene and learn about her from her actions. It takes the fun out of reading by just giving information, rather than letting the reader put pieces of information together in their own mind.

In addition to character descriptions, you should keep an eye out for descriptions of places in your writing, and try to ensure you are showing and not telling what the place is like. The way your characters interact with the setting brings your characters to life, and helps place your readers in the world you've created. Think of the setting as another character, and pay just as close attention to showing, not telling, what a setting in your book is like. Let's look at an example:

Michael could see that the hill was tall, covered in trees, and rocks jutted out even where there was supposed to be a path. He worried that he might not have the energy to make it up the hill.

Okay, that's going to be a tough hill to climb. Hopefully your reader will just want to sit quietly with their book and keep reading rather than attempt to climb this hill. But you can do better than that description, surely. How about this?

Michael was exhausted just looking at the hill. He was going to have to expend a good amount of his flagging energy avoiding the rocks on the barely-visible path, all while being constantly wary of what could be hiding behind the dense trees that covered the incline.

See the difference? The second one puts you a little bit more in Michael's mind, while letting you imagine the vastness of the hill on your own.

Another way to evaluate the effectiveness of your descriptions and whether they are showing and not telling is to consider if you are feeling a connection with the characters' emotions and the associated actions. In the second sentence of the first example, you know Kristy's awareness of being ogled. In the second sentence of the second example, you can sense Michael's exhaustion and his dread at the journey ahead of him. Being wary is very different than just being worried about a few rocks. Neither of the first sentences in the provided examples let the reader connect with the emotions. Instead, they just give a bland statement about the scene. If you can define an emotion that is exuded by a description, even if it isn't explicitly mentioned, then you have likely done a good job of showing and not telling.

As you edit, look for spots in your writing where you mention people, places, animals, and things. Anything that requires a description could possibly be improved by revising your language to show and not tell. This can be a fun part of editing, as it is more writing than editing. As you revise your work, you'll be coming up with new and creative ways to express your characters' stories, their personalities, and even their physical attributes. You'll be flexing your writing muscles, expanding your vocabulary, exploring your imagination, and improving your overall skills.

The second thing to look for in improving your writing when you're editing is the overuse of adverbs, particularly those ending in 'ly.' As mentioned in the beginning of this book, Stephen King famously hates adverbs, excoriating them in *On Writing*. The overuse of adverbs clutters your writing, as adverbs are often redundant, adding nothing to a sentence where you have already shown the reader what they need to know. By adding an unnecessary adverb, you are also telling them something they could figure out just by reading the rest of your sentence. Consider these two examples:

Timmy forcefully threw his phone across the room, angrily aiming for the lamp.

We know Timmy was probably very angry. After all, who throws an item worth hundreds of dollars if they're not angry? The reader is getting the message, but are there extra words in the sentence? And do those words tell us or show us what is going on? Consider this revision:

Red-faced Timmy hurled his phone across the room, the lamp in his crosshairs.

While the first sentence provides all of the necessary information, it also doesn't leave the reader any room for imagination or connection with the words. It tells him or her that Timmy is angry by actually using the word *angrily*. The second version, however, replaces *forcefully threw* with *hurled*, a word that implies the use of force while throwing, showing the reader that Timmy is not just gently tossing the phone. You eliminate an entire word here, and also have the opportunity to *show* anger rather than tell it. Describing Timmy as red-faced rather than using the word *angrily* better sets the scene for the reader, and provides them with insight into Timmy's character. Let's look at another example:

James ran quickly down the road.

and

James ran down the road.

These are two pretty simple sentences, but does the extra word in the first sentence really add anything to what you are trying to convey? Running means moving quickly, so do you really have to say it outright? Here, you have some options. You can leave it as is in the second sentence and let the reader determine in their head how fast James runs, or you can change *ran* to *sprinted* or *jogged,* and truly say what you mean, letting the stronger word indicate whether he was moving his legs more slowly or more quickly. And, in doing so, only use one word rather than two.

Another place to look for overused adverbs in your writing is in dialogue. Do you feel the need to add an adverb after *said* in every line of dialogue? If so, your work is probably scattered with hundreds of extraneous adverbs. Often, the surrounding action of the dialogue and the dialogue itself will indicate how a person is speaking better than an adverb will. Take a look at these:

"I'm so tired," said Deb exhaustedly as she collapsed onto the couch.

"I'm exhausted," said Deb as she collapsed onto the couch.

Does the extra description in the first sentence add anything other than an extra word? The revised version is a tighter, more accurate sentence that conveys your meaning, describes the action, and does so without extraneous words. Action, not adverbs, move a story along and captivate the reader. By eliminating adverbs and focusing on the action you are allowing your story to move along faster, keeping your reader's attention and preventing them from being distracted or bored by unnecessary words.

Commonly Overused Adverbs

- Absolutely
- Actually
- Always
- Basically
- Carefully
- Doubtfully
- Easily
- Especially
- Exactly
- Excitedly
- Extremely
- Fortunately/Unfortunately
- Gladly
- Greatly
- Happily
- Helpfully
- Helplessly
- Honestly
- Hopefully/Hopelessly
- Immediately
- Kind of
- Literally
- Loudly
- Nearly
- Nervously
- Only
- Perfectly
- Probably
- Really
- So
- Suddenly
- Surprisingly
- Thankfully
- Thoroughly
- Thoughtfully
- Totally
- Truly
- Ultimately
- Usually
- Very

When you overuse adverbs, you are taking the easy way out. The English language is rife with strong words that can improve your writing and strengthen your story. Use them. Use your thesaurus, use your own brain, and use friends and family to come up with stronger phrases than an adverb will provide you. If you're editing and hit a spot where you know you can remove an adverb, but the thesaurus and your own brain aren't providing inspiration for a replacement word, yell out to a family member or friend who's around you. Or, shoot them a quick email or text. "Hey, is there another word for *quietly laughed* you can think of?" Even if they don't provide you with the word you are looking for, they may spur some inspiration in your own brain, getting you to the word that works. Just because you're a writer doesn't mean you have to work alone.

As much as adverbs can hurt your work, you don't have to kill every single adverb from your writing. Sometimes, they are necessary. The goal in editing for adverb overuse is to look for the places where adverbs are just you choosing to take the easy way out during the rough draft process. Even if revising a sentence to eliminate an adverb doesn't cut down on the total number of words in a sentence (see the first pair of examples above), it will still improve the overall quality of your writing by forcing you to tap into your vocabulary and imagination. Part of writing is going through various iterations of saying the same thing, just saying it better and more effectively. Exercise those brain muscles, and tap into the creative resources you've cultivated through your years of reading and listening to stories.

Eliminating adverbs can be an effective way to cull unnecessary words from your writing. But removing them isn't the only reason to make your writing more concise, nor is it the only way to do so. Writing concisely can be arduous, as it forces you to think through every word you put down on the page.

Simply put, when it comes to writing, less is more. Strive to be concise. Yes, some writing styles will naturally result in longer sentences and some stories will require more descriptive scenes. However, even if that is your natural writing style, you can still cut unnecessary words and phrases and revise sentences to improve clarity while shortening them. As you're editing to make your writing more concise, begin by looking for descriptions that simply emphasize what is already obvious because of the action taking place. Let's look at an example:

Harold swung the bat, it connected with the ball, and the ball sailed straight over centerfield proceeding over the fence. Harold had hit a homerun. He rounded the bases, waving to the crowd as the team's fans clapped their hands.

Anyone who knows even the basics of baseball would be able to tell from just the first sentence that Harold hit a homerun. There is no need to tell them that with the second sentence. Nor do you need to describe the clapping fans as being the *team's fans*. Presumably, if they are clapping for Harold's homerun, they are fans of the team that Harold plays for. Also, the last sentence contains unnecessary description that the fans were clapping their hands. That is generally what humans clap to express pleasure, correct? Let's try revising the sentences to cut those extraneous words.

Harold swung the bat, and the ball sailed straight over the centerfield fence. He rounded the bases, waving to applauding fans.

See how the action moves along faster without the extra sentence in the middle? The reader still knows there was a homerun, they still know the fans are applauding with their hands, and they still know that the fans are cheering for Harold's team.

Don't be afraid to remove entire sentences or cut entire phrases within a sentence. If you can do so and retain the meaning of the passage, remove it. When you use too many words to say one simple thing you will either come across as arrogant or confused. The best writers—and the best teachers—know how to get the point quickly and clearly. If you can explain a concept simply enough for people to understand, then it is obvious you know what you are talking about. If you can describe a scene concisely then it is obvious you have a clear vision in your mind, and when you put that down on paper effectively the reader will also have a clear vision of the scene.

When editing, look at every word in every sentence with

a critical eye. Ask yourself if every word needs to be there. Do the same examination with paragraphs. If someone doesn't respond in a conversation, do you really need to note that? Or can the reader infer it from the absence of a response? Let the reader infer, and yet again you will have drawn the reader into the story by giving them the opportunity to fill in the blanks rather than over-explaining and boring them.

A few paragraphs ago, we discussed showing and not telling when it comes to description. This is a double-edged sword, because while you want to create a vivid world with descriptions that captivate your reader, you also don't want to overdo it. If you do, you'll bore your reader, killing any hope for succinct, tight writing you had. So, one way to address this problem while still improving your writing is to consider if a description is actually needed at all. Do you really need to elaborate that the squirrel on the street was gray, about a foot long, and had a fluffy tail? Probably not. Most people know what a squirrel looks like, and unless this is a particularly special squirrel that is six-feet tall and is about to murder the families who are living on the street unaware that anything is wrong, the actual physical attributes of the squirrel don't matter.

If all of this deletion sounds depressing, don't despair. Every writer goes through it. It's not unusual for writers to go far beyond the necessary word count for telling a story, only to have it cut down by an editor. Take a minute to mull over this quote from *The Elements of Style*:

> *"Vigorous writing is concise. A sentence should contain no unnecessary words, a paragraph no unnecessary sentences, for the same reason that a drawing should have no unnecessary lines and a machine no unnecessary parts. This requires not that the writer make all his sentences short, or that he avoid all detail and treat his subjects only in outline, but that every word tell."*

If that doesn't inspire you to write more concisely,

nothing we say here will help. That is the most concise, readable way to explain the importance of tight writing. If you have a tendency to be long-winded, print that quote and hang it above your desk. Reread every time you cringe as you start to hit the delete button or take your pen up to cross out a sentence.

Writers write because they have something to say, and they want to say it enthusiastically, which often comes with too many details. That enthusiasm is a good thing! But this is the 21st century, and most people don't have the enthusiasm to read a 700-page tome that their ancestors had before the internet arrived. By deleting unnecessary words, sentences, and descriptions, you make your writing more appealing to today's readers, and you're emulating some of the great writers of days past. Hemingway, anyone?

We discussed the Hemingway App as a tool for editing. If you know you have a penchant for exuberant, lengthy prose that doesn't add much to your story, use this tool as you work on improving your writing with the 'less is more' standard. Even if you only use it a few times, you'll learn how to spot offending sentences and words with ease. After using the app and revising several of your passages, you'll develop a knack for how to eliminate words and rewrite sentences to make them clearer, stronger, and more essential.

As you're trying to make your writing more concise, you should be looking for—and removing—any clichés that you find. It is very easy to succumb to the use of clichés when you're writing a draft. Clichés are easy, they're right at the front of our brains, and they often do the trick to get a point across. We also know that they will be pretty much universally understood, leaving no room for misinterpretation or misunderstanding. However, that does not make them good writing, exciting writing, or even concise writing. If you are using a cliché, there is a better way to say what you need to, and if there's not, then you might consider whether it needs to be said at all. Let's review an example.

Clarence was sleeping like the dead, but his alarm clock woke him in the nick of time, so if he hurried, he could make it to work by 8:00.

Yes, that's a boring sentence overall, but let's see if we can make it a tad more exciting.

Clarence awoke, shaken from sleep by the shrill buzz of his alarm. He rocketed out of bed, determined to make it to work by 8:00.

Just as with adjectives, clichés make you a lazy writer. If you rely on them, you're not reaching for stronger words that add action to your story. Do you see how noting that he was shaken indicates that he was in a deep sleep? If he was just dozing, he wouldn't have been shaken by his alarm going off. We also don't need to use the tired phrase *nick of time* when we say he *rocketed out of bed*, because the reader will pick up on the fact that time was running short for Clarence to get to work because he didn't lazily roll out of bed. By removing clichés, we're also able to better show what is happening in the story. The clichés were telling the reader what was going on, but without them, you're forced to find replacement words and actually create a unique scene. Now, in a sentence that isn't very different in length from the original, we know that Clarence is a deep sleeper and that his alarm is annoying but it saved his day because he hates being late to work. And we know all that without using clichés. When we used clichés we knew that he had to be at work by 8:00, that his alarm went off, and he was sleeping deeply, but did we really care? I sure didn't. Clarence was like any other boring person in that first example. But in the second, we could tell a bit more about his personality because the scene wasn't written using clichés that have been used to describes millions of other rushed morning scenes.

While there are hundreds, likely thousands, of clichés floating around out there, here are a few to jumpstart your brain before you begin lookout duty.

- Busy as a bee
- Like a runaway train
- Fit as a fiddle
- Quick as a bunny
- Tough as nails
- Easy as pie
- Smart as a whip

Now, as you'll notice in the above list, these are all similes. Many clichés are similes, so one way to keep an eye out for them is to look for the words 'like' or 'as' in your writing. When you do, you might be surprised at how many seemingly innocuous clichés wiggled their way into your writing. That's not to say that all clichés are similes, as many can be metaphors, and still other clichés are simply sayings or observations about the world that have been repeated so many times they are no longer insightful. Do any of these sound familiar?

- When the going gets tough, the tough get going
- You only live once
- Plenty of fish in the sea
- It takes two to tango
- Writing on the wall
- Cry over spilled milk
- Better late than never
- Think outside the box
- Selling like hotcakes
- The bottom line
- Taking candy from a baby
- It's not rocket science

We all know what each of those phrases says about the world and the human condition, but none of them make us think. None of them make you go "Huh, interesting idea." All of them lack originality. If you're trying to use your writing to add something to the world, don't repeat the tired old phrases that have been around for decades, or even hundreds of years. Give your unique perspective by using your own language and sentence construction.

Eliminating clichés, showing not telling, improving concision, and ending adverb abuse will go a long way toward making your writing the best it can be. Consider each sentence in the context of these four factors and you'll have an effective strategy for improving your writing. As you go through your manuscript, don't be afraid to delete, and don't be afraid to use original language to convey your world-view. After all, Hemingway did well for himself by being concise, and Shakespeare achieved a bit of fame through inventing new words and phrases for use in his plays.

STEP SEVEN: CHECK YOUR CHAPTERS

For many readers, chapters are how they decide when and where to stop and start reading. It's also how they place themselves within the story, with chapters breaking up scenes and pacing the dramatic action. In a nonfiction book, chapters break up the subject matter into smaller topics, making the book more manageable to digest.

Chapters can be any length, but in general, you should try to keep your chapters within the same range of pages throughout the book. Jumping from a chapter that is two pages long to a chapter that is ten pages long can easily throw off the rhythm of your writing. And, you might find during the editing process that there is a way to work the scene from that two-page chapter into a longer chapter before or after it, improving the action and drama.

Of course, there are some writing styles in which a varied chapter length works. One such instance is if you have short descriptive chapters regularly punctuating longer, action-packed chapters. That is a stylistic choice that can be very effective for telling a story. Ditto if you have shorter chapters for one character's viewpoint and longer chapters for another character's viewpoint. Doing so may even help you better define that character's personality.

If you are writing nonfiction, the approach to breaking up your chapters will likely be a bit different. As you'll notice in this book, some topics require a lot more discussion than others, so their chapters are longer. Likewise, in a book about British royal marriages, Henry VIII's section will be longer than that of any other monarch. And a book about American presidents will probably have a longer section on Abraham Lincoln than on William Henry Harrison. In a nonfiction book, people might skip around and read chapters on the topics they want to understand the most, or that they find most interesting. While it is important to strike a rhythm with an informative nonfiction work, it might be impossible to make your chapters similar lengths if you decided that breaking them up by topic is the most effective strategy. In this case, it becomes especially important to treat each chapter like a mini-book.

One way to approach editing your chapters—fiction or nonfiction—is by editing one chapter at a time. You can do this during another part of the editing process, using the chapters to break up your writing into more manageable chunks, or you can do a separate editing sweep in which you focus on one chapter at time. Always remember to start with the last line of the preceding chapter and end with the first line of the next chapter to see how they connect with the chapter you are currently editing.

No matter which approach you choose, edit each chapter as if it is a mini-book. Most chapters won't stand by themselves as a full story, but they should have a semblance of a beginning, middle, and end that establishes it as purposeful. Don't just randomly make a new chapter every ten pages or every 2,000 words. How you space your chapters can improve, or hurt, the pacing of your story. Be deliberate about spacing, and make your chapters matter.

In the section on the electronic resources, we mentioned the Scrivener program. Scrivener is helpful for tracking chapter length, as it tracks the word and character count of your manuscript by section. If you're not using Scrivener to write, there are a couple ways to check the length of your chapters to make sure they aren't all over the place. One option is to go through your manuscript on the computer, manually highlighting each chapter and using a word count feature. You can also take a printed manuscript and split it up into chapters, arranging each chapter into an individual pile and comparing them by size. This might not be the most scientific of methods, but it gives you the rough estimation you need to tell if you're way off base on your pacing.

The one thing that you must do no matter how long or short your chapters, or how you pattern their lengths, is to make sure they begin and end with a compelling sentence or two. Of course, you should be trying to make your entire book compelling, but it is especially important for your chapter beginnings and ends to be strong and effective at moving the story along. So how do you edit for that?

When looking at the beginning of a chapter, make sure that the transition from the last chapter makes sense right off the bat, or that you explain the new setting immediately. You do not want your reader to be lost. This means letting the reader know they're now in a different place than they were a page ago, so they best be ready for the action. Did you end the last chapter in an abandoned city lot? Great, start the next chapter with a sentence about the beautiful meadow the scene will be set in. Or, if you are still in a city lot, but moving to a new character's viewpoint, try out a line of dialogue from the new character as the first line. That way the reader is instantly clued in to the change in viewpoint without just being told "This is Harry's chapter, not John's." Of course, there is always the stylistic option of heading your chapters with a place and date, name and date, or name and place, but that's for you to determine if it makes sense with the type of book you are writing.

Editing the end of a chapter is a bit different from editing the beginning. The end of a chapter needs to give the reader a reason to turn the page. It should make them want to keep reading, while also providing a sense of closure for the chapter's scene. However, don't make every chapter end like a soap opera episode, with a cliffhanger. It will become tiresome for the reader, and with each chapter you'll have to come up with progressively more exciting cliffhangers and first lines of chapters to keep the momentum going. That's really not possible, and it will make your story stale and cheesy. You can think about a chapter's last line or two as someone leaving a room dramatically. Remember the Seinfeld episode where George learns that it's best to just leave a social situation on a high note, so every time he makes someone laugh he leaves? The concept is similar for ending a chapter, except it's not always about laughter. But it is about a good stopping point to leave the reader wanting more.

One trick for editing the end of a chapter is to review the last sentence as written, consider ways to revise it to make it more impactful, and if nothing seems right, take a look at the second to last sentence. There's a possibility this should actually be your last sentence, and you were just too long-winded to recognize it. It's the same concept as editing the beginning of your novel to see if you started it out too early in the story. It's also possible to run well past the necessary ending of a story, whether that be at the end of a chapter or the end of the book itself. Remember our earlier discussion about not being afraid to cut out entire sentences? In editing the ending of chapters, you have an opportunity to trim unneeded fat to strengthen your book. That's not to say this is always going to be the solution, nor will it always be necessary, but it is one possibility for making the end of a chapter more effective.

Now, it should probably go without saying that the first sentence of your first chapter and the last sentence of your last chapter are the most important sentences in your book. Yes, classic books have a lot of great lines scattered throughout, but does anyone ever make a list of The Best Literary Quotes from Page 53? No, it's often the first lines and the last lines that are immortalized. Don't believe that last lines can be as memorable as first lines? Try these last lines on for size:

The Great Gatsby: "So we beat on, boats against the current, borne back ceaselessly into the past."

Gone With The Wind: "Tomorrow is another day."

Pay attention to your chapters. Pay attention to your endings. Your readers will be paying attention, and those are the people you need to keep happy.

STEP EIGHT: PROOFREAD

By this point, you've done the larger pieces of editing. You've done the pieces that require you to change words, revise sentences, and move around entire paragraphs or chapters. You've looked at your chapters, made sure your acronyms are consistent, and you've considered your character arcs. Through all of that, you probably fixed some spelling errors and comma errors, too. But now is the time to dig in deep and really put on those detail-oriented glasses. It's proofreading time.

Why do you wait to proofread until later in the editing process? Well, while you are making revisions you are likely spotting and fixing smaller errors like spelling mistakes—as you should—but you probably didn't catch them all. Then, while you were rewriting, revising, and moving pieces of your manuscript around, you likely created new errors that need to be fixed. No one is perfect, and that includes writers and editors. It doesn't make sense to proofread first, and then go through and make potentially significant changes to sections of writing, then have to go through and proofread it all again. Instead, if you lightly proofread while you're working on the larger edits, you will only need to go back and do one heavy proofread.

Proofreading is different from editing in that you are

looking for actual errors, not ways to improve the art of your writing. Some of the errors you are looking for may be typos, others may be grammatical errors, but they all need to be fixed. How many times have you been reading a book, even one published by a reputable publishing house, and noticed a missing word? It's happened to most of us at least once, and it is always disconcerting. You need to do a careful proofread, no matter how many times you have spellchecked because there are many, many details that can easily be overlooked. While your goal in proofreading is to not miss a single error, let's be honest—chances are good you are going to miss at least one. Chances are good you've found one (or more) in this book! But you need to be as careful as you can while proofreading, and the best way to be careful is to approach proofreading with an idea of common errors to look for, but be open to errors at anytime, anywhere, and in any form. Even an error in spacing should catch your eye during the proofreading process. That's how detailed you need to be.

One strategy for remembering what to look for as you proofread is to make a checklist to keep by your computer or by your printed copy. Include common errors on the list, as well as errors that you know you routinely commit. Everyone has different habits in their writing, and your common errors will be different than your favorite author's common errors. They might misuse semicolons, and you might always type *the* as *eht*. However, use your checklist only as a guide. Don't become so committed to it that you miss other errors. Be focused on everything that is on the page. Be focused on every word, every sentence, and every punctuation mark. That is the only way you are going to catch errors.

So what are some of the common errors to put on your list?

The first one we'll go over might sound like it belongs in the improving your writing phase and it certainly can go there! Catch any error you can, whenever you can. But when you're proofreading, you're more likely to be paying attention to punctuation, and it's in paying attention to punctuation that you are going to catch the dreaded run-on sentence. Run-on sentences are the enemy of succinct, clear writing. How do you identify a run-on sentence? Will adding a period in the middle of a sentence that is free of punctuation split that sentence into two separate, complete sentences, each with a subject and verb? Maybe!

Or, conversely, look for a lot of commas. If you spy a sentence with more than two commas in it, see if there is a way to chop it up into more than one sentence. Sometimes, you will have a sentence with more than one comma that is not a run-on and that's fine. But follow your grammar guide and common sense to determine if you really need to keep that sentence going as one long sentence. It's easy to fall into the habit of just typing until your idea is completed, resulting in long-winded sentences even when you are revising your work.

The proofreading phase should also include careful attention to the story's timeline. Do the dates make sense? Are people waking up with the sun in the east and going to bed with it setting in the west? When you were editing and revising, it's possible that some of your timeline got out of whack, or details that shouldn't be in a certain scene ended up there. Keep your eyes peeled for details that seem out of place as you proofread. There's a good chance they stick out for a reason—they don't work where they are, or they simply don't belong in the story anymore because of revisions you made.

Many of the other items to proofread for are the common errors we covered earlier in the book, but it's worth another mention to make sure you don't miss them. These are the errors that are easy to make, that can derail a sentence or a paragraph, distracting the reader and demeaning your reputation.

If you've already run spellcheck, you've likely found typos like *eht* in place of *the*, but there's no guarantee that you didn't just click past it, hitting *Ignore* and leaving the typo to languish in your manuscript. When you're typing fast, things get by you. It's just part of writing a long-form work. If you are questioning something, don't just move on. Look it up! English grammar is complicated—sometimes unnecessarily so—but there are rules that you need to abide by if you are going to be taken seriously as a writer.

You're also going to want your grammar references for checking punctuation usage during the proofreading phase. Commas can be killers when it comes to grammatical excellence, and when you are proofreading you should also be watching for a lack of commas. Your style guide should have a handy section on comma usage that can guide you when you are unsure what to do. Remove one? Add one? Change it to a semicolon or a dash? Check one of your handy resources.

While commas are certainly a common punctuation to watch for, don't get so distracted by commas that you ignore other potential punctuation errors. Do you use an apostrophe in a word that's meant to be plural, not possessive? What if it's a plural possessive, is the apostrophe in the right spot? Don't just skim—pause when you see an apostrophe and consider if it's being used properly. Not to mention, whenever you see the word *it's* or *its*, double-check that apostrophe or lack thereof.

Another easy punctuation error to make is using the wrong quotation mark around dialogue. If you've hit the space bar wrong, or simply made other changes to dialogue there's always the possibility that one of your quotation marks will be facing the wrong direction. Watch for this. Depending on the font you are using it might be subtle and difficult to notice, but if you are looking for this error you will find it.

As you're editing for apostrophes, commas, quotation marks, and the rest of the punctuation gang, take a look at the spacing between sentences and between punctuation. Make sure there is a space after a comma, after a period, and after all other punctuation marks. Don't put a space between a comma at the end of a quotation and the closing quotation mark. When we're writing, we're not paying attention to formatting, and it's easy to not hit the spacebar as hard as you thought and just keep typing without noticing the lack of a space. Ignore those kinds of errors at your own peril when proofreading. It might seem small, but if there is a missed space on a page, it will stick out like a sore thumb when your book goes to print. The entire page will look off, and your reader's rhythm will be thrown off when they hit it.

In addition to punctuation errors, you should keep an eye out for capitalization. As we discussed in the chapter on editing for consistency, there are hard and fast rules surrounding capitalization. Do not capitalize seasons. The seasons are always lowercase (unless they are at the beginning of a sentence, of course), but months and days of the week should always be capitalized.

Another common capitalization error is capitalizing directions. If you are writing about the direction a character is driving, they are headed *north*, not *North*. But, if they are headed to Georgia, and don't want to let their family know their specific location, they could say they are heading to the *South*. Ohio is in the *Midwest*, but it is to the *east* of Indiana. A good rule of thumb is to consider the specificity of what you are referring to when determining if it should be capitalized or not. And of course, look it up in a style guide or grammar guide.

Don't just look for instances where you have capitalized a word erroneously, though. Also look for instances where you have not capitalized a word that should be. Are all of your characters' names capitalized? Are names of cities and states? What about stores and schools?

While you may have caught errors in tense and word usage during an earlier read of your book, it never hurts to keep an eye out for awkward sentences, subject-verb disagreement, or improper tense usage. Double check your use of words like *was* and *were* and similarly simple but easily misused terms.

Prepositions are another example of seemingly simple

words that are easy to misuse. A common way to misuse a preposition is by simply mistyping. This is especially true for prepositions that are only a letter different from one another. Even though you know the proper usage of *on* and *in*, it's very simple to type *riding on the car* when you meant *riding in the car*. One slip of the finger can change a calm scene into a scene about a Sunday drive straight out of *National Lampoon's Summer Vacation*. It's also easy to miss these kinds of errors when you are proofreading, because your spellcheck will miss the error since *on* is an actual word and that sentence still makes sense. Likewise, if you're not reading carefully, your eye won't catch the word as wrong because it is an actual word.

What you do not need to edit or proofread for, in regard to prepositions, is whether your sentences end in them. Unless, of course, the sentence is poorly constructed on the whole, but don't blame the poor little preposition for all your troubles. But, wait! You've heard your entire life that it is wrong to end a sentence in a preposition, so what is this madness? No, we're not trying to pull the wool over your eyes. In fact, we'll cite a source to prove it to you. As Mignon Fogarty, the Grammar Girl, explains in *Grammar Girl's Quick and Dirty Tips for Better Writing*, "...nearly all grammarians agree that it's fine to end sentences with prepositions, at least in some cases." So what are the cases you should be editing for? As with adverbs, it's the unnecessary prepositions that you need to keep an eye on. But if you don't need the preposition, get rid of it. For example, "Where did you go to?" is not okay to ask. But "Where did you go?" is okay to ask. Unless, of course, it's character dialogue and that's how the character speaks.

Speaking of short and seemingly simple words, look for instances where you may have misused *a* and *an*. The general rule is to use *a* before a word that starts with a consonant, and *an* before a word that starts with a vowel (and sometimes an *h*—just keep it consistent). When you're typing fast it's easy to miss hitting the *n* on your keyboard, or to hit it when you don't mean to. Heck, you might even get so into what you're writing that you add a *d* onto *an* and you end up with a conjunction! See how easily things can get off the rails when you're in the heat of the moment and filled with inspiration but not with a desire to focus on keyboarding? Pay attention when you see *a* and *an* crop up in your writing, and make sure you are using the correct one. It's important to remember that *an* should be used before words that start with a vowel sound. It is the sound that governs whether you use an *a* or *an*. And, sometimes, you use an *a* before a word that starts with vowels.

Examples:

I went to school to get an MBA degree.

They talked about it for over an hour.

We need to have a united front.

She had a unique doll collection.

If you are using acronyms, it's important to remember to listen to how an acronym sounds (like the MBA example above). Another example would be: *I work at an HIV clinic.* And, to really show the difference:

She was an NBC reporter.

He was a NATO member.

You also need to be sure you're using the same version of words for which there is more than one acceptable spelling. Likely, you've trained yourself over the years to use just one spelling of a word like color, and that choice was probably determined by whether you prefer American or British spellings, but that doesn't mean you won't occasionally slip up. As with *a* and *an*, even if you know which spelling is correct and which you should be using, your typing fingers can do their own thing. That is how you can end up with a *theatre* when what your book needs is a *theater*. A situation that might be applicable to only a few writers, but is worth bringing up nonetheless, is if you are an American writer writing a book that is set in England, or vice versa. Which version of *color* or *colour* do you use? *Humor* or *humour*? You need to determine your preferred version, and which one matches up best with your story and its style and setting. Then stick to it, and edit to make sure you did stick to it throughout the entire book.

When proofreading, also look for errors that aren't necessarily in the text. Huh? Yes, your book is going to include parts that aren't in the actual body of your text. Even if you're writing fiction, you'll likely have a table of contents for your chapters. Be sure that your chapter titles and the order of the chapters make sense, first of all. Then make sure they match up correctly with your table of contents. Before you begin the formatting process it isn't worth putting page numbers in the table of contents, but making sure your chapter titles are arranged correctly at this point will make that process much easier. It will also give you the opportunity to ensure your chapters are titled properly. You also need to look at chapter titles for consistency. Are you italicizing all of them? Either do or don't. Or italicize those that are for a specific character's viewpoint, and bold those for another character's viewpoint. Just keep it consistent. Also, determine what you're doing with shorter words like *a, the, and, to* when they appear in a chapter heading. Are you capitalizing them or not? What did you do with those shorter words in your title? When you're proofreading you need to look for all of these things.

As we mentioned in the chapter on editing for consistency, taking breaks are important when doing this type of work. You need to maintain a certain level of concentration, and if you feel that slipping away, stand up and take a break. Go for a short walk, or read a chapter of a light book. Even if you don't feel your concentration slipping away, take a break every hour or so. If you don't, you might be unknowingly losing concentration. These types of breaks are important throughout the self-editing process, but are especially crucial when you are staring at one word at a time, looking for errors that are hiding in the midst of thousands of words.

Every little detail really does matter, and the more you are able to correct, the more professional your book will be. It might sound tedious to proofread for everything from an extraneous comma to a missed space, but the time and strained eyes are worth the effort when you don't have any Amazon reviews stating that your book was "lazily thrown together" or "a good story, but the typos were distracting."

Proofread. Proofread well. Proofread more than once.

STEP NINE: PRINT IT

You may have already printed your work once before, choosing to mark edits and corrections on a hardcopy of the work earlier on in the editing process. If you've done this, you've also gone back and made the changes on your computer version of the manuscript. If you haven't made the changes yet, go do that now.

Okay, now that your changes are made on the computer, print your manuscript again. If you haven't printed the work for a read on a hardcopy yet, do it now. The words will look different when they are printed out than they do on the screen, and you will have a brand new perspective with words on paper. You also won't have the distractions of the internet, Facebook notifications, or emails popping up around you when not on a computer screen.

If you have already printed your manuscript once to edit, you will need to look at your work on a hardcopy again to review the changes you made to the computer version. You will find things on the printed page that you did not see on the computer screen. This is a guarantee.

When you are preparing your document to print, consider putting it in a different font than you would usually read. It should still be something easily readable, don't go crazy and put it in some fancy script. It should just be a font that you don't normally use, so if you prefer Times Roman, try Courier. Doing so will make you read more carefully, because you won't be overly familiar with the font. You could also try making your work a different font every twenty pages, or making every chapter a different font. Use different colors for the type if you want. As long as you're not changing the words on the page, it doesn't really matter what font or color the words are. The point is to trick your brain into paying attention. You are trying to avoid the tendency to skim, which is an even greater tendency after you have written, read, rewritten, and reread your work. Another tactic to help you focus while reading a printed document is to enlarge the font. Sure, it might take you some extra paper to print it out in size 16 font, but you will be able to see errors more quickly than you would if you were fighting with your eyes to determine if there's a space or two after a period. Everything will be magnified on the page, causing errors to jump out at you, giving your eyes and your brain a break. But that's not an excuse to start skimming! It's just a way to catch more errors.

While you are reading the hardcopy, you can also use a straight edge to ensure your eyes don't wander and you're not skipping lines. Since you already know the story, possibly by heart at this point, you won't feel like you're missing anything if you skip a line or two, and you might not notice you skipped the lines. By grabbing a ruler or a blank piece of paper, and moving it slowly down the page, line by line, like you used to when you were first learning how to read, you will be forced to pay attention. Another option, similar to using a straight edge, is to use your finger or a pen and deliberately move it from word to word as you work. If you are really trying to force yourself to focus, use the pen to make a tiny dot above each word you read. In doing so, you won't be able to just drag it along the paper while your eyes are skipping over words.

Take your proverbial red pen (or actual red pen) and

mark up the printed manuscript as you are doing this edit. Do this, and only this. Don't have your computer screen open. Just mark up the printed document until you have made it through the entire manuscript. Then, flip it back to page one, fire up your computer, and start making the edits you have marked down on the printed manuscript. The major benefit of this method is that you will be going through your manuscript in its entirety yet again while you make changes page by page. The downside is that this is time-consuming. Also, it's possible you might miss one of the edits you marked down on the printed page. To avoid missing any edits, take breaks in between pages, or, after you finish making an edit, circle it on the page. That way you can easily see at a glance if you've made all the changes you intended to. In contrast to these potential downsides, a major benefit of this tactic is that you are away from your computer for a long period of time. This is especially helpful if you're someone who is easily distracted. If you are, then setting up shop with nothing but a stack of paper, a grammar reference book, and a red pen or two might be the most efficient and effective way for you to do a comprehensive, near final, edit and proofread.

The second option is to edit and proofread your manuscript a chapter at a time on printed paper, then go in and edit on the computer between each chapter. This breaks up the process a bit, and while it will take you just as much time in the end, it may seem less time consuming. It will also help you consider each chapter as a standalone scene, perhaps giving you additional insight into the important beginning and ending sentences of those chapters.

A third option is to edit on the computer as you find errors on the printed page. You can do this either a page at a time, or each individual error at a time. However, it is still smart to mark down the edits you are making on the printed paper. That way you have something to reference if you have a question later on. It also gives you an extra layer of consideration about the change. As we've discussed before, taking an extra beat when you are editing and proofing is always a good idea. The primary downside to making changes directly on the computer as soon as you spot an error on the printed page is the constant back and forth. If you are someone who works better on the computer, who is not easily distracted, and who may not have the patience for yet another re-read, then option three might be the one for you. Just take it slow, and still use a straight edge to keep you focused on the printed page.

At this point, you will likely not have too many major edits to make, having done those earlier on in the process. The purpose of printing out the manuscript is to help you notice the little things, the errors that are easy to miss on a laptop screen when your eyes are tired or you're so sick of the story that you just start skimming. It might seem like there can't be anything left for you to catch at this point, but as you'll find, that's not going to be the case.

STEP TEN (OPTIONAL): READ IT BACKWARD

Now, you've got a cleaner copy of your manuscript because you've carefully combed through a printed version and made the required edits on your computer version. If you've reached this stage and feel confident the book is as good as it will get, feel free to stop. But could you have still missed something? Of course. So if you feel inclined, you can take the time to read your manuscript backward. This may sound crazy, but it's effective.

When you're reading backward, you cannot pay attention to the story development, so you won't. You'll be reading everything you've written in a completely new order, seeing the words as words alone, and the sentence and punctuation use as formatting alone. As a result, you'll notice things like misplaced apostrophes, commas, and spaces where no spaces should be. It's especially effective to read backward if you take a break from your manuscript, so you don't have the words intuitively in your head because you've stared at the pages for weeks on end. Take a week or so away from the work until you pick it up to read backward. Your eyes will thank you, too.

Before you get started on this task, let's clarify what it means to read backward. It does not mean that you read every single word backward. That would be yzarc. It would also be time consuming, confusing, and not at all useful. Instead, flip to the end of your manuscript and put your eyes on the last sentence. Read the last sentence normally, from beginning to end. Make any edits you think are necessary. Then move up to the second-to-last sentence. Do the same. And so on and so forth. If you're reading a paper copy, use a straight edge or a pen pressed on the words to keep your place. If you're reading on the computer, it might be a bit more difficult to keep your place, but you'll be able to make edits directly. To make reading backward on a computer easier, zoom in on the pages so that you only see a few at a time. This way, your eyes won't stray up to the next line as easily, and your eyes won't have to work as hard on what is going to feel, at least at first, unnatural.

If one sentence at a time is a bit overwhelming and you feel yourself getting distracted or confused, read bigger chunks at a time, normally. For example, you can read the entire last page in normal order, from first word to last word. Then, you can move on to the second to the last page, doing the same. The entire point of reading your manuscript this way is not to give your brain a confusing workout, but to give you the opportunity to see your words in a different light. Perhaps most obviously, it makes you go slower. If the sentences or pages don't make any sense in the order you are reading them, then there's no rush to move to the next sentence or page to find out what happens next. It prevents you from getting emotionally attached to your characters again, and attaching meaning to the words that might prevent you from changing or deleting them. If you read the word *very* when you're reading backward, it won't seem as necessary as when you are reading forward and it seems crucial to emphasizing just how fat the crime boss is. Working slowly, with your words in a new order, should allow you to pinpoint errors you wouldn't otherwise notice.

By the time you are reading your manuscript backward, it should be mostly clean. Your characters and plot are fully developed, most typos are cleaned up, and grammatical issues are largely fixed. Reading backward is the last step in a long process, and it gives you one final opportunity to pick up on even the smallest, most camouflaged of errors.

PART III:
THE FINISHED PRODUCT

At some point, no matter how much you love the book you have written, no matter how nitpicky you are, you are going to get tired of it. Reading the same thing several times in a row, particularly after you have written the original version, gets tiring. Reading it backward is going to take you a while, and may feel brutal. The constant reading and re-reading and marking up gets repetitive and boring. It also means that you'll either miss things, or start over-editing if you keep going. Because at a certain point, you just won't care—even though you know you should.

If you get tired of editing early on in the process, that's understandable, too. But at that point, just set the book down for a bit longer and give yourself a break. If you're going to self-edit and self-publish, you need to do it right, so you can't stop just because you're tired of looking at your words.

However, you can stop if you've read, re-read, re-written, re-read, and read your work backward. You can stop if you are now finding about one comma every dozen pages that is making you question your grammatical skills. No one is perfect, and no one is going to catch every single error in a long manuscript. Also, you're going to drive yourself crazy trying to follow every single grammar rule in the English language perfectly in every sentence you write. First of all, it's not even necessary for a fiction book, particularly one that includes dialogue, and second of all, there's a good chance it's not even possible to write a compelling book and follow every grammar rule under the sun.

If you keep editing after you have made a full effort, diligently seeking out typos and word choice errors, eliminating clichés, and evaluating your character and plot development, you might end up making your writing weaker. If you are literally hunting for errors, you will begin imagining them, and you will be reading your work in a way it was never meant to be read. Unless you're writing the next major classic, it's more than likely most readers will only read your book once. That's not to diminish the importance of a solid editing job, but to demonstrate that you are viewing your book through a much different lens than the average reader by the second time you've gone through it, never mind the fifth or sixth time. This isn't an excuse to be lazy—it's a reason to stop editing when you believe you have done all that you can to make your work solid, clean, and professional.

Should you hit a point where you think you're done editing, but you're not quite sure, take yourself out of the equation. Ask a friend or family member whose eagle eyes and opinion you trust to take a look through the manuscript. Let them know you're not looking for stylistic pointers at this juncture (unless you really want to torture yourself) but are hoping they will point out any glaring errors, plot holes, or other issues they see with the manuscript. If they balk, you can even ask them to skim it, and let you know if they find any glaring errors in the first few chapters.

Take a look at what the people who did a full read through have to say about your work, and if there is nothing major that they've pointed out, make adjustments where you agree they need to be made, and then stop. If they point out places where your character answers to the wrong name or that you have a run-on sentence on every other page, then you should probably continue editing.

For those people who have only agreed to skim your work, typos and other errors are going to be harder to find given the number of times you have already gone through your manuscript. However, if they do find some, especially if they are only reading a portion of the book, that's problematic and is an indication that you are not done. It's not an indication, though, that you need to rework your plot or deal with character development again. Unless, of course, they point out something they noticed amiss with either of those things. If you don't have family or friends that you can approach to help you out in this way, or you're simply just not ready to let someone close to you read the work yet, the internet can help you out. There you can connect with beta readers.

Beta readers will sometimes do the work for no cost, just for the promise of a free read. Or, they might be a college student looking to get some editing or reviewing experience. Either way, it's free feedback and another set of eyes to help. So where do you find these internet angels? Writers' forums are an excellent source for finding beta readers.

Goodreads.com, a thriving community for readers and appreciators of the written word, offers a beta readers group to help connect authors with someone to read their book. The group also offers this astute disclaimer about beta readers:

"Avid beta readers are not your editor or proofreader and don't expect them to do the grunt work. That's up to you. But they could have spotted a few fleas BEFORE you released the book and helped strengthen your story."

The Goodreads beta readers group has nearly 10,000 members and active message boards on which authors can post the genre of their book and a request for a beta reader. Authors can also offer to pay for a beta reader.

If you don't find what you're looking for in a beta reader on Goodreads, check out writing.com or absolutewriting.com, both of which have opportunities for you to connect with a beta reader. You might also consider posting an ad on your local Craigslist page, or putting up a notice at your local library. People who live in large cities or areas near universities might have better luck with this tactic than those in rural locations, but it can't hurt to try. You never know what a retired English teacher, literature student, or other writer might be looking to do in their spare time. Unlike using an internet-based beta reader, if you find a local person willing to read your work there is the opportunity to meet up in a coffee shop and have an actual conversation about it. If you are the kind of person who would enjoy such a conversation, this could be enormously helpful.

When you're selecting a beta reader from the internet, consider not only their willingness to read your work, but if they are the target audience for your book. Are you writing a YA adventure mystery? Do you want a fifty-year-old woman with no children who says her favorite genre is historical romance to read and critique your book? Probably not. What about a fifty-year-old woman who was a third grade teacher and says the *Nancy Drew* series helped shape her appreciation for reading? She would probably be an excellent match for your book. The goal here is to find someone who can give you productive feedback on your plot, characters, and overall story.

If you're putting out a request for a beta reader for a nonfiction work that you have written, your inclination might be to see if you can find an expert on the subject matter you've written about. However, unless you are writing a technical, in-depth work whose target audience is people in the field of the subject you've written about, this is probably a bad idea. If you send your manuscript to an expert in the subject matter, they likely have a long-established perspective on the topic that might be quite different from yours, resulting in a slightly biased beta read. As with fiction, you should look for a beta reader who is in your general target audience.

When you get comments back from a beta reader, don't take every single one of their critiques as gospel. Use your judgment when deciding what changes to make to your manuscript. You should also steel yourself against criticism. After you've poured your heart, soul, and time into writing and editing a book, it can be tough to hear someone doesn't think it's as strong as you think it is. But everyone has their own opinions of what makes good writing and what makes a compelling story. You are asking for someone's opinions and insight here—it is up to you to decide how to use the information you get from them. Value their perspective, but don't take everything they say to heart. This is your work. Everyone you approach for insight into your book is going to have a different suggestion or observation, so knowing when to stop asking, and when to ignore certain suggestions or criticisms, is important to finding your stopping point.

If you wanted to, you really could edit forever. There is no such thing as perfection in writing, and if you strive for it, you will never publish your book. Your readers aren't going to be perfect, so you don't have to be either. Your work should be polished and professional, but perfection is unrealistic. When you are satisfied that your work is as error-free as it can be, you are done. You are ready to start the formatting, publishing, marketing, and selling part of self-publishing. Congratulations!

Conclusion

By the time you have decided to set down your book and stop editing, you probably will have done a significant amount of rewriting. You have put a lot of work into making your writing the best it can be, and you've probably learned quite a bit about yourself, your work ethic, your focus, and your writing style along the way. That's all good, and it will all benefit you in the future as you pursue more writing projects.

Every step of self-publishing a book is labor intensive. Self-publishing might sound easy enough at first blush, but the fact of the matter is you have to be committed to doing it right to do it well. It is not as simple as once copying and pasting what you've written into an internet program, selecting a few options about page size and cover design, clicking your mouse, and *bam* there's your book on Amazon. Ah, if only it were that simple. Of course, you can make it that simple, but don't be shocked when your book drifts into a sea of other titles never to get noticed. No one has a manuscript that is ready to go on the first draft, and even a draft that's been revised once is inevitably going to have errors, often large ones. The self-editing portion of the self-publishing process is essential for ensuring you are putting out a final product you can be proud of. It might take months to self-edit properly, it might give you a headache or several, but to build up your reputation as a writer, self-editing correctly is critical.

That's why following careful, deliberate steps for editing and proofreading is so important. Shortcuts won't work. In this book, we've laid out the basics of self-editing and the steps to follow. You may find that the steps in the order we've laid out don't necessarily work for you. That's okay. Mix and match and move them around. Just be sure you are paying attention to all of the elements we've laid out.

The most important part of editing is focusing. You must remain focused on the details and know what you are looking for. Just reading and re-reading through your manuscript isn't enough. You need to be deliberate, and you need to be taking notes, interacting with the words, considering what is on the page. Treat it like a senior thesis. Every time you get tired or bored of editing, consider that someone will be seeing your name attached to the final product, and consider how it reflects on you if there are errors throughout the book. If you want to establish yourself as a writer, you need to cultivate a reputation for attention to your craft. That means editing well.

To edit well, you can't go it entirely alone. Self-editing does not mean using just your brain to edit. It means saving large sums of money by not paying someone else to edit your work. It means a little bit of money for the right resources to make sure your editing is done right. The resources we described at the beginning of this book will become lifelines for you, and they are absolutely worth the investment, not just for this specific project, but for any writing you are doing going forward.

Self-publishing, when done well and done right, can propel your writing career. Not everyone is going to have the commercial success of the initially self-published *Fifty Shades of Grey*, but with a good product, a marketing strategy, and a few sales, good reviews will follow and from there more sales will come. To have a good product to start with, you must do a thorough editing job.

If self-publishing a book is not just a side hobby for you, but a way to supplement an already established or nascent writing career, it is also imperative that it be as professional as possible. As a writer, you are likely trying to convince people to hire you or publish your work, and if they Google you only to find a self-published work full of errors and sloppy writing, why would they think they could trust your work? You can also use your work as an example of your editing skills to seek out future editing or proofreading jobs. This is especially possible if you've saved earlier versions with tracked changes, showing how you worked through the process to improve the writing. See? Self-editing does have rewards that make the time commitment and the blurry eyes worth it.

Even knowing that there are rewards from self-editing awaiting you at the end of the long process, you might find yourself tired and discouraged at certain points. That is okay, and it is to be expected. Should you find yourself in this situation, the best thing to do is to set down your red pen and your manuscript, and take a long break. Quality over speed every time. Don't immediately give up on self-editing and start searching for editors to hire online. Instead, take some time and breathing room to separate yourself from the project. If you have been dedicating a portion of every day to editing, you could find yourself burned out very easily, especially if you aren't a detail-oriented kind of person. It's also easy to get discouraged if you are finding many errors, even if they are just typos. But remind yourself that this is why you are editing, and that this happens to every single writer without fail. No first draft is perfect. No second draft is perfect. Editing is a long process, no matter who the writer is. So take walks, take days off, heck, take a week or two off. Every time you take a break and return to your manuscript you will have new energy and a new perspective. The quality of your work will benefit from you giving yourself a break.

Self-editing carries with it a great responsibility, but it is absolutely worth the time and the inevitable frustration. You will come out of the process a much-improved writer, with a keen grasp on your strengths and weaknesses. You will be able to edit faster and more effectively the next time you sit down to write a book, and you will have at least a few hundred more dollars in your pocket than you would if you had hired an editor. Put that money toward a cover design or professional formatting, and your book could be headed for self-published success.

As you complete your work, and are looking for advice on the remaining steps in the self-publishing process, turn to the rest of the advice that Kennebec Publishing offers for self-publishing authors. There are many details to take care of, and it never hurts to have a little extra guidance from people who have been there. Visit us at www.KennebecPublishing.com.

Happy editing, and happy publishing!

www.ingramcontent.com/pod-product-compliance
Lightning Source LLC
Chambersburg PA
CBHW071312040426
42444CB00009B/1988